Weeks Ringle and Bill Kerr

QUILTS
TRANSPARENCY

10 Modern Projects

Keys for Success in Fabric Selection

From the Modern Quilt Studio

C&T PUBLISHING

PUBLISHER Amy Marson

CREATIVE DIRECTOR Gailen Runge

EDITOR Lynn Koolish

TECHNICAL EDITORS Helen Frost
and Gailen Runge

COVER/BOOK DESIGNER Kristy Zacharias

PRODUCTION COORDINATOR Jessica Jenkins

PRODUCTION EDITOR
Alice Mace Nakanishi

ILLUSTRATOR Bill Kerr

Style photography by Jim White

Flat quilt and sample photography by
Christina Carty-Francis and Diane
Pedersen of C&T Publishing, Inc.

Published by C&T Publishing, Inc., P.O. Box 1456, Lafayette, CA 94549

Ringle, Weeks.

 Transparency quilts : 10 modern projects : keys for success in fabric selection : from the Modern Quilt Studio / Weeks Ringle and Bill Kerr.

   p. cm.

 ISBN 978-1-60705-354-5 (soft cover)

 1. Quilting--Patterns. 2. Patchwork--Patterns. 3. Color
in textile crafts. I. Kerr, Bill, 1965- II. Title.

 TT835.R556 2011

 746.46--dc23

                          2011026616

Printed in China

10 9 8 7 6 5 4 3 2

ACKNOWLEDGMENTS

It's a standard thing to thank one's editors, but we'd like to say something different. We've been just amazed by all the people at C&T Publishing. In addition to our wonderful editors, Susanne Woods (acquisitions editor) and Lynn Koolish (developmental editor), we've been so impressed with everyone else we've dealt with at C&T. Kristy Zacharias, our book designer, has been so enthusiastic about our work, and we are grateful that she designed a book that shows our quilts to their best advantage. The marketing people, the publicity people, the people who ship our books, and of course Amy Marson, the publisher, work hard to make us look good and create opportunities for us. We are truly grateful for their energy and intellect.

We also feel lucky to be able to work with our photographer, Jim White. Jim's attention to detail and lighting is evident in the styled shots in this book, and we are grateful for his expertise.

Mickey Sweeney and Thom Barthelmess, along with their respective sweet dogs, were gracious enough to let us take over their beautiful homes for our photo shoots. We are indebted to them for their generosity and support.

Our fabulously talented intern, Jane Arvis, a student at Dominican University, is a whiz at both sewing and graphic design. In addition to cutting countless yards of fabric and piecing some of the quilts in this book, Jane also helped with yardage calculations and color variations in the pattern section. We are grateful that Dominican University made it possible for Jane to work with us.

Thanks also to the always hardworking Sandra Vega, who has been particularly helpful with cutting and preparing kits. In the midst of this book and a myriad of other projects, Sandy has been a calm and reliable presence.

Our daughter, Sophie, has become a great helper in our studio in addition to being a delightful energy in our lives. Sophie also generously lent us her pink bedroom for the *Sweet Talk* photo shoot. Thanks, Sophie!

CONTENTS

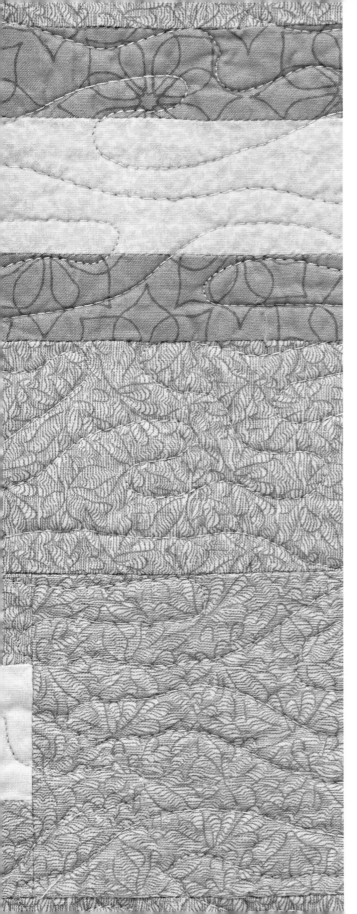

INTRODUCTION

We love color, but we love the visual relationships among colors even more. At workshops we teach, we sometimes ask students to choose their least favorite color; then we watch in fascination as they come to love that same color when it's in a palette with other colors. Developing palettes with which to make beautiful quilts does not require fancy gizmos or prescribed formulas. It takes a basic understanding of color theory and a bit of focus when buying fabric. Our hope is that with this collection of quilts, you will begin to see color in a new way and grow in your understanding and appreciation of color in the process.

Many quilters associate quilting with individual blocks. They love a particular block pattern, so they make a lot of blocks from that pattern and sew them together to make a quilt top. We have always had a different method of designing. We focus less on the individual blocks than on the relationships among all the pieces of the quilt. You'll notice that some of the quilts in the book use block construction and others don't. Going back and forth between design, color theory, and construction is endlessly fascinating to us. It was through this interest that we began creating designs with pieces that, when viewed as a whole, give the illusion that one color is overlaid on another. We refer to these quilts collectively as *transparency quilts*.

In architecture, interior design, and product design in the past half century, there has been a focus on making materials seem lighter and more airy. Houses that used to be constructed from stone and wood can now be built as glass boxes that appear to float on the landscape. Televisions that used to be massive pieces of furniture are now thin enough to hold in the palm of your hand.

Similarly, the color options for quilting textiles were extremely limited until the mid-twentieth century. Advances in printing technology and textile production have given twenty-first-century quilters color choices unimaginable to previous generations of quiltmakers. Without such wide varieties of fabric available, we would never have been able to conceive of transparency quilts.

Making transparency quilts requires time to think about color in a new way. We hope this book will help you refine your understanding of color theory and give you a new perspective on how some of your favorite fabrics might be used in a new way. We also hope that you might rethink some of your assumptions about fabrics that may appear to lack potential but in fact can play an essential role in achieving the effect of transparency. Mostly, we hope this book will inspire you to take a little time to play with color options before you start your next project, because every project is an opportunity to learn something new.

Making transparency quilts requires time to think about color in a new way.

TRANSPARENCY

UNDERSTANDING COLOR

The beauty of the concept of transparency is that it is not just a technique for a certain style of quiltmaking. Whether you love modern or traditional quilts, scrappy or understated palettes, there's a pattern that will work for the fabrics that you love to use.

To be able to select the fabrics that will achieve the look of transparency, you'll need to understand the basics of color theory.

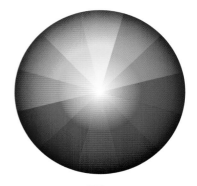

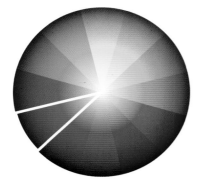

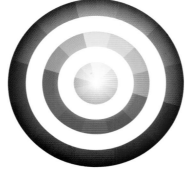

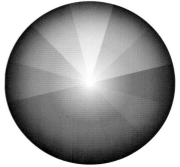

HUE is the technical term for "color." A hue can be used to describe a group of colors, such as "blues." On the color wheel above, the hues appear on the spokes.

VALUE describes the lightness or darkness of a hue. Understanding value is critical to being able to select the right fabrics for transparencies. The lightest value of each hue is at the center of the color wheel; the darkest value is at the outer edge. We've divided the color wheel above into light, medium, and dark values of each hue.

SATURATION is another way to describe the brightness of a hue. A saturated hue might be described as a "bright blue" while a less saturated blue might be called a "dusty blue" or a "gray blue." The top color wheel shows saturated color in a value range from lights to darks. The bottom color wheel shows the same hues desaturated.

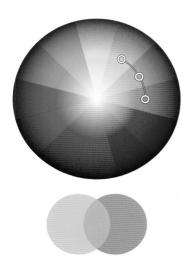

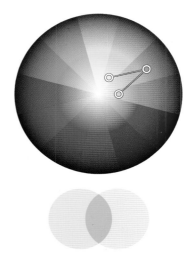

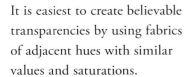

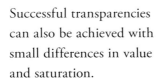

It is easiest to create believable transparencies by using fabrics of adjacent hues with similar values and saturations.

Successful transparencies can also be achieved with small differences in value and saturation.

What most often causes a transparency to fail is having one saturation or value that is far more intense, darker, or lighter than the others.

The remainder of this chapter explores how to create successful transparencies.

CREATING TRANSPARENCIES

Yellow Plus Blue Doesn't Have to Equal Green

It's understandable to think that transparencies have to be literal to be visually convincing. For example, you might think that if you're trying to develop a transparency with yellow on one side and blue on the other, the overlay section needs to be green. Surprisingly, that's not necessarily the case.

That's because having the exact hue is not always what makes the transparency convincing. In most cases, it's the value that will make or break the effect. If you get the value right, you

can experiment with hues, and you might find that a broader range of colors than you imagined will look convincing. Also, the form of the piecing will help trick the brain into imagining transparencies. Look at this overlap in *Share and Share Alike*. It is clear that there are two squares overlapping.

Color Balancing in Transparencies

When developing a transparency, look carefully at the colors you're considering. In most cases there is one color in particular that you want to work with—look at its hue and saturation. When you choose the second and third colors, stick with a saturation and hue that are similar to those of the original color you chose. Think of the transparencies as a musical trio. One musician who plays too loudly will drown out the others. Conversely, one who plays too softly will not be heard. You can work with any hue, any value, and any saturation, but the companion fabrics need to look as though they are part of the trio.

Dominant Transparencies

If you're working on developing your transparency and you're not happy with the results, it's probably because the transparency doesn't look balanced. Is one fabric too dark? Is one too bright? Does one look like the odd man out?

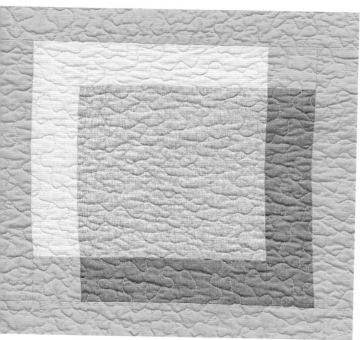

From *Share and Share Alike* (page 30)

Developing a Color Variation

Making a color variation of any transparency quilt in this book requires understanding the original color relationships. We'll explain these relationships as we walk you through making *Madras* (page 54) in a different color palette, in this case brown and orange.

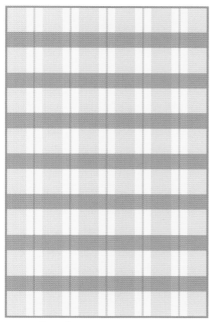

Original *Madras*

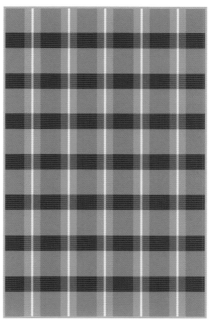

Brown *Madras*

The original *Madras* is predominantly blue. The horizontal stripes are medium blue and the field is a lighter value of that same blue. Note that although the field is lighter, it is the same hue as the horizontal blue strips. It does not become more blue green or blue purple.

Center blue best matches original hue.

To adapt this pattern in brown and orange, first choose a brown fabric for the horizontal stripes. This fabric, like the blue in the original, will be the darkest value in the quilt.

Dark brown

Next, find a lighter brown for the field fabric, making sure it is similar in hue to the first and that it doesn't seem to be a greener or redder brown than the original.

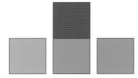

Center brown best matches original hue.

Now select a hue for the vertical stripes. Here we've chosen burnt orange.

Burnt orange

The fabric used where the brown horizontal and burnt orange vertical stripes overlap should create a believable transparency. Think of it as the result of blending the brown and the burnt orange. Its value should fall between the values of the dark brown and the lighter orange. Make sure the saturation is not more intense than that of either of the stripes.

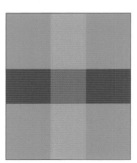

Transparency

Now select a hue for the narrow vertical accent. Here we chose a light tan.

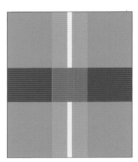

Light tan

To make a convincing transparency, we selected a darker value of that tan for the intersections.

Darker tan

FABRIC SELECTION

Using Prints

Although some of the quilts in this book were made with solids or tone-on-tone fabrics, others were made with medium- and small-scale prints. Prints can be used to create transparencies, but they require a careful eye to make the illusion visually convincing. Prints can be a little trickier to select because they look so different in your hands than they do from a distance.

As you're selecting fabrics, try to pile them up under or near a good light source and look at them from a distance. If the fabrics are still on bolts, place them in the order in which they would appear in the transparency. When you look at them from across the room (we call this "the ten-foot rule"), try to notice whether or not the relationship among all the fabrics looks balanced. Do some combinations appear to have a closer relationship than others? You want your eye to move back and forth among them and not feel as though any part of the transparency looks heavier or lighter than the entire composition.

Choosing a Field Color

Some of the quilts in the book have a field or background color. Selecting the background color is important to the feel of the transparency. If the transparency is particularly delicate, avoid using a saturated solid or a high-contrast print for the background because it will distract from the subtle colorwork that you've established in the transparency.

If you are considering a solid or tone-on-tone fabric for your background, look for one with about the same level of saturation as found in the fabrics chosen for the blocks. It can be a different hue, as in *Share and Share Alike* (page 30), but the subtlety of the colorwork will disappear if the field or background fabric seems visually overpowering.

If you have print fabric in mind for the field, try auditioning smaller prints with less contrast than the fabrics in the transparency. You might look for an overall value that is decidedly lighter or darker than the transparency you're developing.

WHAT DOESN'T WORK AND WHY

Although the block shown here would work fine in a garden-variety quilt, it does not work as a transparency block because it is visually unbalanced. Creating transparencies requires establishing a relationship among the fabrics so it appears as though light is hitting the quilt in a particular way. This visual deception can be created with any kind of fabric, but the hierarchy among the fabrics must be clear. In this block, the contrast of the red-and-orange print overwhelms the delicate colorwork of the more subtle yellow and orange prints. Used with different prints, the red-and-orange print would be fine, because this technique is all about context and establishing visual relationships among the fabrics. If one fabric jumps out too much, the viewer notices the jump, not the relationships among the rest of the fabrics.

Unsuccessful transparency

Sample Palettes

We can talk abstractly about color theory, but quilters have the challenge of dealing, in most cases, with fabrics that are not solid. Whether you plan to use batiks, prints, yarn dyes, or hand dyes, you will need to be able to figure out how to create transparencies with the fabrics available to you. To help, we've put together a series of palettes that we hope will demonstrate combinations of fabrics that work to create a convincing transparency, some that don't work, and why.

Palette 1

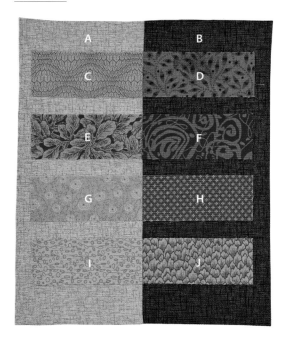

Note that there's a significant value contrast between Fabric A and Fabric B. Fabric B is much darker than Fabric A. The fabrics used to create a transparency don't need to have this same degree of value contrast; in fact, the contrast is greater here than in some of the other palettes we'll show you.

In Palette 1 you can see that pairs C–D, E–F, and G–H are different hues but share the same degree of value difference as pair A–B, so the transparency is convincing visually. Fabric I, however, is too similar in value to the base fabric, Fabric A—it disappears a bit into the background, so even though the value relationship between I and J is good, Fabric I doesn't read as well as it could when placed next to Fabric A.

It's also worth mentioning that although this is an analogous palette, the fabrics are monochromatic prints, and they are small to medium in scale. Fabric F, for example, has just two values of orange in it, and the motif is not large. There's no complementary color, say a blue or green, in any of the fabrics. Although we'll show some multicolored palettes later, transparencies with tone-on-tone fabrics are easier to design than those with high-contrast, larger-scale patterns, which entail more colors to manage. So if all this color theory talk sends your eyes rolling back into your head, start with an analogous palette of low-contrast, small-scale prints.

Palette 2

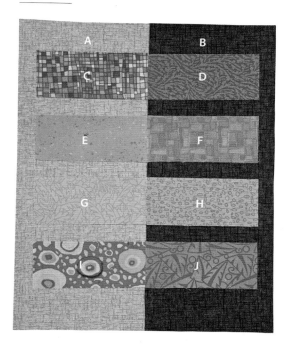

Palette 2 uses the same background fabrics as Palette 1 (Fabrics A and B), but it has a different group of transparency fabrics. When we first looked at Fabric C, we didn't think it would work because of its tiny flecks of white. After we cut it up and saw it with the rest of the palette, though, we decided it was fine. Having the white next to yellows and golds seems to temper it visually, but if it were navy and white, for example, it would definitely not work. Fabric pair E–F works well, but we thought that Fabric G was a bit too saturated compared with the rest of the palette. From a distance, in a finished quilt, Fabric G is the one that would always seem visually jarring. Similarly, Fabric I is the only one in the palette with contrasting colors, so it doesn't work.

Palette 3

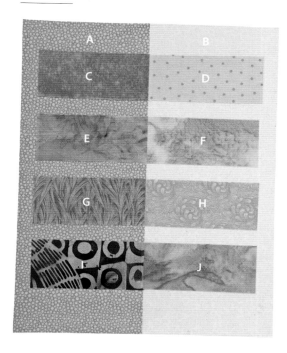

Palette 3 has a softer look because the contrast between the background fabrics (pair A–B) is less than the contrast in the two previous palettes. As a general guideline, a greater value difference between the background fabrics makes for a more dramatic quilt. In contrast, this more subtle value difference suggests a calmer palette. Although the transparency pairs are different hues, the value shifts among them are similar, so the transparency is visually pleasing. When our eyes reach Fabric I, however, the contrast of the black-and-beige print destroys the illusion of the transparency. Fabric I is so high in contrast compared with Fabric J that its print prevents the viewer from seeing the transparency.

Palette 4

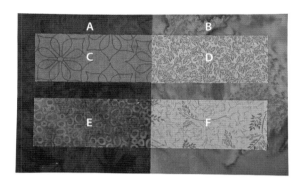

Palette 4 has a hue-shift problem. The value contrasts between Fabrics C and D and between Fabrics E and F would be fine if viewed in black and white. Fabric C would work if Fabric D had a little more green in it. When you set up a clear blue palette, it doesn't work well to suddenly throw in a blue that has a green hue in it. The blue-green fabric needs a fabric with more green to play with. The transparency of Fabrics E and F is convincing because they are the same hue.

Palette 5

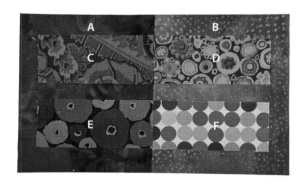

Now we're moving to those tricky larger-scale, multicolored prints. They can make really fun transparencies, but they require a little more attention than the easygoing tone-on-tones. In Palette 5 we see a good pairing between Fabrics C and D. Both have similar hues and although both are multi-colored, the value shift between them is clear. Fabric F is the troublemaker here. Although we were able to get away with that little bit of white in Palette 2's Fabric C, Fabric F in Palette 5 is not playing well with others. There's just too much contrast between the white spaces and the colored dots in the print. The white takes over visually and the lovely colorwork between Fabrics C and D is lost.

Palette 6

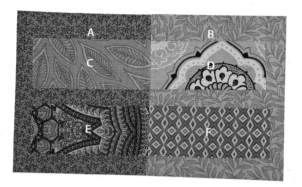

In Palette 6 we meet the Motif Bully. Although the large-scale motif in Fabric E gets along with the smaller motif in Fabric F, Fabric D is determined to steal the show. The high-contrast motif with a black line next to a lighter green motif makes it visually challenging to see the colorwork. As soon as you try to look at the colorwork of the transparency, that motif is screaming "Hey! Over here!" It's a beautiful fabric but doesn't work with the rest of these more subdued prints. The other problem with Fabric D is that its background color is too close to that of Fabric B, so it's hard to see the edges of Fabric D. The definition of the motif is stronger visually than the edge of the block, and that's confusing to the viewer.

Palette 7

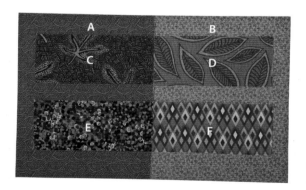

Palette 7 shows the range of saturation that you might consider in a quilt. If you were to look at just these six fabrics, Fabric F looks too bright and saturated among these softer reds. If, however, you were to think of the fabric pairs C–D and E–F as representing either end of a spectrum from less to more saturated, and you were to make sure that all the other fabrics in the palette were in this range of brightness, both pairs would be fine.

QUILTS

MINT JULEP

Aromatic sprigs of mint inspired the forms of this summery quilt. The subtle transparency is in the vertical strips, which act as stems, linking together the leafy palette of blues and greens.

Skill/Time INTERMEDIATE

The large number of pieces and the use of templates for cutting require a bit more time to make this quilt, yet *Mint Julep* is straightforward for a careful quilter.

Materials

All fabric calculations assume a width of 42".

	WALL/BABY	NAPPING	FULL/QUEEN
FINISHED SIZE	38" × 52"	50" × 76"	89" × 104"
MATERIALS NEEDED			
Light blue fabric for stems and binding	½ yard	¾ yard	1 yard
Medium blue fabric for stems	¼ yard	½ yard	1 yard
Assorted blue and green prints for leaves	¼ yard each of 6 fabrics for a total of 1½ yards	⅓ yard each of 8 fabrics for a total of 2¾ yards	½ yard each of 11 fabrics for a total of 5½ yards
White field fabric	1½ yards	2½ yards	5¼ yards
Backing	1⅝ yards	3¼ yards*	8¼ yards*
Batting	44" × 58"	56" × 82"	95" × 110"

* Pieced crosswise

Tip The fabric requirements show the minimum number of blue and green prints needed, but the scrappier the better. We used small amounts of 22 different fabrics from our stash in the quilt shown.

Cutting

PREPARING THE TEMPLATES

Trace the patterns for Templates A, B, and C/D (page 109) onto template plastic. Cut them out and label them. Put a piece of double-faced tape or a loop of clear tape on the back of each to keep it from slipping as you cut.

CUT	WALL/BABY	NAPPING	FULL/QUEEN
FROM LIGHT BLUE FABRIC			
1¼″ × 1¼″ pieces	24	52	152
1¼″ × 5½″ pieces	6	8	16
FROM MEDIUM BLUE FABRIC			
1¼″ × 4½″	27	56	160
FROM ASSORTED PRINTS			
A trapezoids, using Template A	54	112	320
FROM WHITE FIELD FABRIC			
Divider strips	2 strips 1½″ × 52½″ *	3 strips 1½″ × 76¼″ *	7 strips 1½″ × 104¾″ *
2 side panels	5¼″ × 52½″ *	6¼″ × 76¼″ *	6¼″ × 104¾″ *
B trapezoids, using Template B	48	104	304
C right-facing ends, using Template C/D	6	8	16
D left-facing ends, using Template C/D	6	8	16

* Cut pieces marked with an asterisk from the lengthwise grain.

MAKING THE QUILT

Assembly

1. Using a ¼″ seam allowance, sew alternating light and dark blue pieces to form the stem strips. Press the seams open.

Piece stem strip.

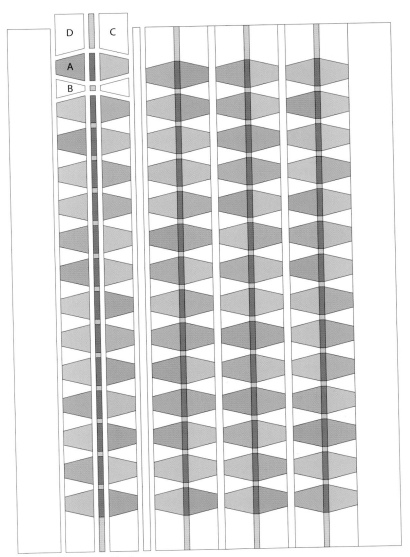

Napping quilt assembly diagram

2. Align the right side of a downward-pointing white B trapezoid with the right side of an upward-facing colored A trapezoid. They are properly aligned when their side edges overlap ¼″ away from their flush edges. Sew together. Press the seams open.

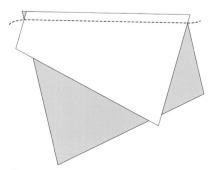

Align A and B trapezoids.

3. Repeat for all but 8 trapezoids for the napping quilt (6 for the wall/baby and 16 for the full/queen). These will be sewn to white end pieces.

4. Arrange the pieces, referring to the quilt assembly diagram (page 25) as needed. Evenly distribute the various leaf fabrics. Rearrange pieces if you notice clusters of lights or darks or identical fabrics across from each other. Number the pieces with chalk to keep them in order when taking them from the layout area to the sewing machine.

5. Sew the leaf fabrics and white end pieces into columns. Press the seams open.

6. Sew the columns, stems, divider strips, and side panels together. Press the seams open.

Finishing

For information on quilting, batting, and binding, see Quilting and Batting Options (page 102) and Binding (page 104).

1. Layer the top, batting, and backing; then quilt.

2. Bind.

SIZE VARIATIONS

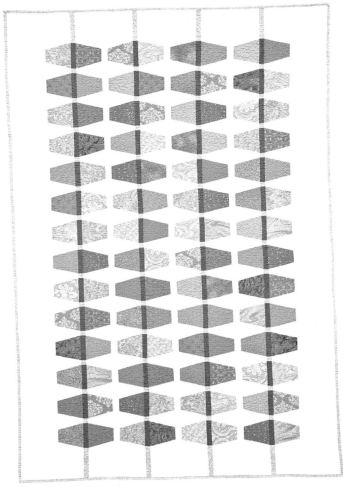

Napping quilt, 50″ × 76″

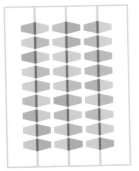

Wall/baby quilt, 38″ × 52″

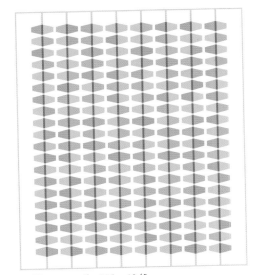

Full/queen quilt, 89″ × 104″

DESIGN

Fabric Selection

We used a wide variety of blues and greens in various scales. Some motifs were small, others much larger. None of the fabrics were high-contrast prints because these would have competed visually with the form of the pieces.

Note range of hues and range of scales in prints.

Light and dark stem fabrics

Quilting

We densely stippled the stems and leaves using a medium blue-green thread in both the top and bobbin. The white background is quilted less densely with white thread. Using a blue-green thread for both the top and bobbin thread created silhouetted forms of the stems and leaves on the white backing, like a cast shadow.

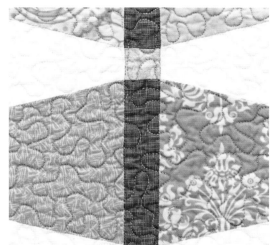

Stipple quilting

COLOR VARIATIONS

Notice how the stems of the first two variations with dark fields get lighter rather than darker as they pass through the leaves. The stems of the final variation follow the lead of the original design, darkening in the center of the leaves.

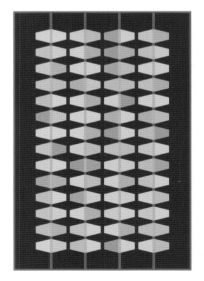
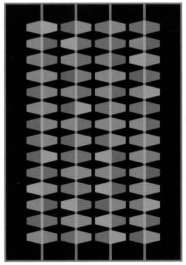
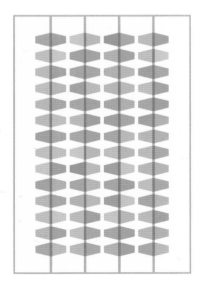

SHARE AND SHARE ALIKE

If, like many quilters, you give away most of the quilts you make to friends and family, consider making this project for yourself. We love the ease of construction that makes this a manageable bed quilt. The colors can be easily adapted to fit any home.

Skill/Time
ADVENTUROUS BEGINNER

This is a sophisticated quilt, yet the cutting and piecing are simple enough for a beginner. Because it uses just four fabrics, you can easily explore custom colors by stacking bolts on top of each other to make choices confidently.

Materials

All fabric calculations assume a width of 42".

	WALL/BABY	NAPPING	FULL/QUEEN
FINISHED SIZE	44" × 57"	57" × 82"	88" × 107"
MATERIALS NEEDED			
Center square fabric	¾ yard	1¼ yards	1¾ yards
Darker fabric	¾ yard	1 yard	1¼ yards
Lighter fabric	¾ yard	1 yard	1¼ yards
Field fabric	1½ yards	2½ yards	6 yards
Binding	½ yard	¾ yard	1 yard
Backing	3 yards*	5 yards	8¼ yards*
Batting	50" × 63"	63" × 88"	94" × 112"

* Pieced crosswise

Tip When selecting fabrics, note that the center square fabric doesn't have to be the exact color you would get if you actually mixed the colors of the lighter and darker fabrics together. The overlapping squares give the viewer a clue to expect the transparency, which is in turn supported by, but does not rely solely upon, the colorwork.

The light and dark outer pieces are joined at right angles. To ensure that they read as a single L-shaped piece, avoid directional fabrics. Allover, small-scale prints or solids hide seams well and are good choices.

Cutting

CUT	WALL/BABY	NAPPING	FULL/QUEEN
FROM CENTER SQUARE FABRIC			
A pieces	4 pieces 7½" × 23"	5 pieces 7½" × 41"	7 pieces 7½" × 41"
FROM DARK FABRIC			
B pieces	4 pieces 2¼" × 23"	5 pieces 2¼" × 41"	7 pieces 2¼" × 41"
D pieces	1 piece 9¼" × 28"	2 pieces 9¼" × 28"	2 pieces 9¼" × 41"
FROM LIGHT FABRIC			
C pieces	4 pieces 2¼" × 23"	5 pieces 2¼" × 41"	7 pieces 2¼" × 41"
E pieces	1 piece 9¼" × 28"	2 pieces 9¼" × 28"	2 pieces 9¼" × 41"
FROM FIELD FABRIC			
F pieces	2 pieces 2¼" × 28"	4 pieces 2¼" × 28"	4 pieces 2¼" × 41"
Vertical divider strips, 2¾" × 11"	8	18	28
Horizontal divider strips	3 strips 2¾" × 36½" *	5 strips 2¾" × 49¼" *	6 strips 2¾" × 62" *
Top and bottom panels	2 pieces 4¼" × 44" *	2 pieces 4¼" × 56¾" *	2 pieces 10¼" × 88" *
2 side panels	2 pieces 4¼" × 49¼" *	2 pieces 4¼" × 74¾" *	2 pieces 13½" × 87½" *

* Cut pieces marked with an asterisk from the lengthwise grain.

MAKING THE QUILT

Making the Strip Sets

The strip assembly method simplifies the piecing. We've incorporated extra length into each strip to allow for slightly ragged edges to be trimmed flush.

1. Using a ¼″ seam allowance, make the center square strip sets by sewing all the A, B, and C pieces together as shown. Press the seams open.

Center square strip set

2. Make the light edge strip sets by sewing an F piece to each E piece. Press the seams open.

Light edge strip set

3. Make the dark edge strip sets by sewing an F piece to each D piece. Press the seams open.

Dark edge strip set

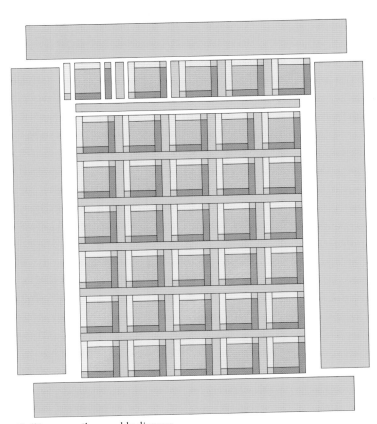

Full/queen quilt assembly diagram

Cutting the Strip Sets

	WALL/BABY	NAPPING	FULL/QUEEN
7½"-wide center square units	12	24	35
2¼"-wide light edge units	12	24	35
2¼"-wide dark edge units	12	24	35

1. Cut the center square strip sets into the specified number of 7½"-wide units.

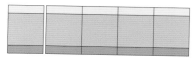

Cut center square units.

2. Cut the light edge strip sets into the specified number of 2¼"-wide units.

Cut light edge units.

3. Cut the dark edge strip sets into the specified number of 2¼"-wide units.

Cut dark edge units.

Making the Blocks

	WALL/BABY	NAPPING	FULL/QUEEN
Number of blocks	12	24	35

Sew a light edge unit and a dark edge unit to either side of each center square unit, pinning carefully through the seams first to ensure precise alignment. Press the seams open.

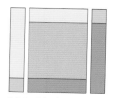

Make blocks.

Assembly

1. Piece the blocks to the vertical divider strips to form rows, referring to the quilt assembly diagram (page 33) as needed. Press the seams open.

2. Sew a horizontal divider strip to the bottom of each row *except* the bottommost row. Press the seams open.

3. Align the rows precisely, using chalk to mark guidelines from the vertical divider seams down across the horizontal divider strips. Pin the next row on the chalk lines; then piece the rows together. Press the seams open.

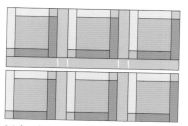

Make chalk guidelines for alignment.

4. Sew on the side panels. Press the seams open.

5. Sew on the top and bottom panels. Press the seams open.

Finishing

For information on quilting, batting, and binding, see Quilting and Batting Options (page 102) and Binding (page 104).

1. Layer the top, batting, and backing; then quilt.

2. Bind.

SIZE VARIATIONS

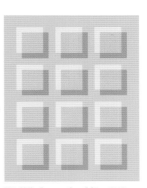

Wall/baby quilt, 44″ × 57″

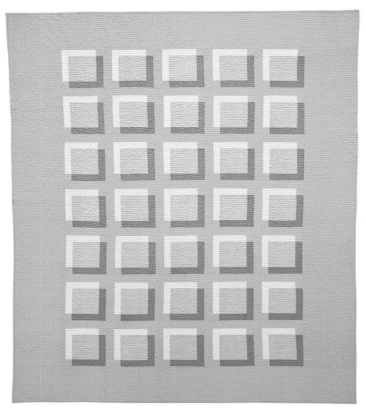

Full/queen quilt, 88″ × 107″

Napping quilt, 57″ × 82″

WHISPER

The softness of these hand-dyed solids from Cherrywood Fabrics creates gentle color combinations. Each pairing of circles and squares creates a different amount of transparency—sometimes subtle, sometimes more evident.

Whether you're insetting circles for the first time or have already mastered the art of sewing curves, you'll find these semicircles easy to handle.

Materials

All fabric calculations assume a width of 42".

	WALL/BABY	NAPPING	FULL/QUEEN
FINISHED SIZE	38" × 50"	50" × 75"	88" × 100"
MATERIALS NEEDED			
Assorted solids	½ yard each of 8 fabrics	½ yard each of 13 fabrics	1 yard each of 14 fabrics
Binding	½ yard	¾ yard	1 yard
Backing	1⅝ yards	3⅛ yards*	8¼ yards*
Batting	44" × 56"	56" × 81"	94" × 106"

* Pieced crosswise

Tip When laying out the quilt, avoid putting two highly contrasting semicircles or two highly contrasting rectangles together in a block. Pair dark with dark, light with light, light with medium, or medium with dark, but never light with dark. Such a pairing would draw attention to half of the block rather than the whole block and would be visually jarring. It is fine to have the circles and rectangles contrast with each other, though.

Cutting

Trace the patterns for Templates A and B (page 108) onto template plastic. Cut them out and label them. Put a piece of double-faced tape or a loop of clear tape on the back of each to keep it in place as you cut.

CUT	WALL/BABY	NAPPING	FULL/QUEEN
FROM ASSORTED FABRICS			
6¾″ × 13″ rectangles	24	48	112
A semicircles, using Template A	24	48	112

MAKING THE QUILT

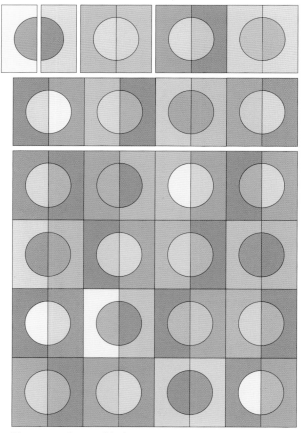

Napping quilt assembly diagram

Preparing the Rectangles

1. Fold a rectangle in half crosswise. Align Template B to the folded fabric *with arrows pointing to the fold.* This is critical—the template must be oriented correctly.

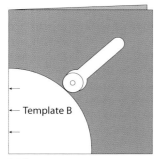

Make sure arrows are pointing to fold.

2. Cut along the curve of Template B. Remove the semicircle. (You won't be using these semicircles in this quilt; set them aside so you don't get them confused with the A semicircles you've cut out already.)

3. Repeat Steps 1 and 2 for all the rectangles.

Assembly

1. Arrange the pieces, referring to the quilt assembly diagram (page 40) as needed. Rearrange pieces if you notice distracting patterns such as clusters of lights or darks, or identical fabrics side by side. Number the pieces with chalk so they won't get out of order when you take them from the layout area to the sewing machine.

2. Pin each semicircle into its corresponding rectangle by first folding the 2 pieces in half and finger-creasing to mark the centers. Place the semicircle faceup on a table. Now turn the rectangle upside down so the right sides are facing. Align the center creases at their edges and pin at number 1. Next pin at numbers 2 and 3. Finally pin at numbers 4 and 5, the midway points on the curve. You can find those points by folding points 2 and 3 to point 1 in the center and creasing.

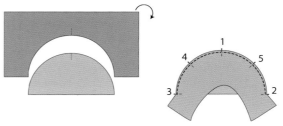

Match right sides together; then pin in sequence.

3. Using a ¼″ seam allowance, piece each pinned semicircle–rectangle pair together. With the semicircle right side up, sew the pieces together slowly, maintaining a ¼″ seam allowance. If you sew it with the semicircle facedown, the rectangular piece will pucker under the semicircle as you sew. Press the seams open on the back and then press the finished piece again from the front.

4. With right sides together, sew the 2 pieced halves of each block together, pinning carefully through the seams first to ensure precise alignment. Press the seams open.

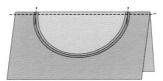

Pieced block

5. Pin the blocks into rows and sew. Press the seams open.

6. Pin the rows together and sew. Press the seams open.

Finishing

For information on quilting, batting, and binding, see Quilting and Batting Options (page 102) and Binding (page 104).

1. Layer the top, batting, and backing; then quilt.

2. Bind.

SIZE VARIATIONS

Full/queen quilt, 88″ × 100″

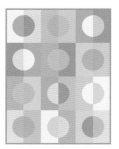

Wall/baby quilt, 38″ × 50″

Napping quilt, 50″ × 75″

DESIGN

Fabric Selection

While you could easily make all the circles light and the back-ground squares dark (or vice versa), mixing light circles on dark and dark circles on light makes *Whisper* more dynamic. We avoided extremely light or dark fabrics so as not to make the quilt too stark. Working with a limited color and value palette concentrates the design on differences of value rather than differences of hue, further accentuating the transparency.

The fabrics used in *Whisper* have a wide value range but avoid extremes.

Quilting

We chose plain stippling to unite the field fabric. This creates a background on which the inset circles float. The freehand spirals in each circle relax the otherwise strict geometry of the piece.

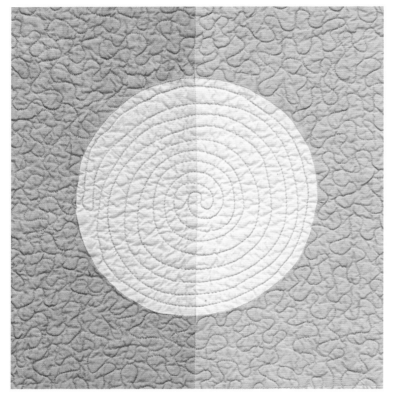

Stipple quilting

Spiral quilting

COLOR VARIATIONS

We selected Cherrywood hand-dyed fabrics for their gentle, suede-look colorings. These colors and the subtle transparency they created together led to the quilt's name, *Whisper*. Here are three more *Whisper*-like variations.

 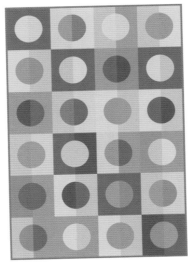 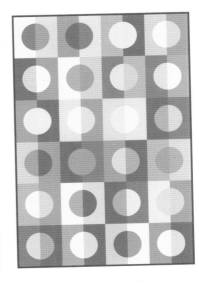

HELLO SUNSHINE

Hello Sunshine combines gentle colors and sophisticated overlays to produce a contemporary quilt with a classic feel. Imagine for a moment a yellow lattice set over an orange set of squares: You see the yellow dissolve into peach as it overlaps the orange. But there's a twist—at the center of each orange square the lattice becomes luminous yellow, bringing light to the center of each square.

Skill/Time INTERMEDIATE

Hello Sunshine's small pieces require a little extra time for careful cutting. Small cutting errors that are inconsequential in quilts with large pieces can add up to trouble with smaller pieces, which stretch less and are not as forgiving.

Materials

All fabric calculations assume a width of 42″.

	WALL/BABY	NAPPING	FULL/QUEEN
FINISHED SIZE	40″ × 49″	49″ × 78″	87″ × 106″
MATERIALS NEEDED			
Yellow lattice fabric	1½ yards	2 yards	4 yards
Light orange lattice fabric	¾ yard	1 yard	2 yards
Medium orange square fabric	¾ yard	1½ yards	3¼ yards
White fabric	1 yard	1¾ yards	3½ yards
Binding	½ yard	¾ yard	1 yard
Backing	2⅝ yards*	3¼ yards*	8¼ yards*
Batting	46″ × 55″	55″ × 84″	93″ × 112″

* Pieced crosswise

Tip Careful handling of the long, narrow divider strips in the napping and full/queen sizes will minimize accidental bowing or distorting of the strips. If you find it hard to cut the strips out of a single piece of fabric, you can seam together two shorter lengths.

The outer yellow border around the quilt is cut 2½″ wide but will be trimmed to 1¾″ wide after quilting. This extra width allows you to trim the quilt nice and square despite any warping that might occur in the handling and quilting of the piece. With wider borders, this distortion is usually not very noticeable, but this border is so narrow it needs the extra leeway.

Cutting

CUT	WALL/BABY	NAPPING	FULL/QUEEN
FROM YELLOW LATTICE FABRIC			
Top and bottom panels	2 pieces 2½″ × 41½″ *	2 pieces 2½″ × 51″ *	2 pieces 2½″ × 89″ *
Horizontal divider strips	4 strips 1½″ × 41½″ *	7 strips 1½″ × 51″ *	10 strips 1½″ × 89″ *
Vertical edge pieces, 2½″ × 9″	10	16	22
Vertical divider pieces, 1½″ × 9″	15	32	88
Strips for strip sets	5 strips 1½″ × 33″	10 strips 1½″ × 33″	20 strips 1½″ × 41″
FROM LIGHT ORANGE FABRIC			
Strips for strip sets	4 strips 3¼″ × 33″	8 strips 3¼″ × 33″	16 strips 3¼″ × 41″
FROM MEDIUM ORANGE FABRIC			
3¼″ × 3¼″ squares	80	160	396
FROM WHITE FABRIC			
1½″ × 3¼″ pieces	80	160	396
1½″ × 4¼″ pieces	80	160	396

* Cut pieces marked with an asterisk from the lengthwise grain.

MAKING THE QUILT

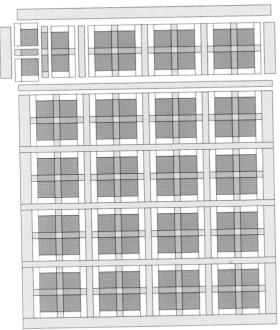

Wall/baby quilt assembly diagram

Making the Strip Sets

	WALL/BABY	NAPPING	FULL/QUEEN
A strip sets	2	4	8
B strip sets	1	2	4

1. Using a ¼" seam allowance, sew a yellow strip to a light orange strip to make an A strip set. Press the seams open.

Make A strip sets.

2. Repeat to make the required number of A strip sets.

3. Sew 3 yellow strips and 2 light orange strips together as shown to make a B strip set. Press the seams open.

Make B strip sets.

4. Repeat to make the required number of B strip sets.

Making the Blocks

	WALL/BABY	NAPPING	FULL/QUEEN
A units	40	80	198
B units	20	40	99
Finished blocks	20	40	99

1. Cut the A strip sets into the required number of 1½"-wide A units. Set these aside.

Cut A units 1½" wide.

2. Cut the B strip sets into the required number of 1½"-wide B units. Set these aside.

Cut B units 1½" wide.

3. Sew a 1½″ × 3¼″ white piece to each medium orange square. Press the seams open.

Join fabrics.

4. Divide these pieces into 2 equal stacks. To form corner units, sew a 1½″ × 4¼″ piece to the left side of each orange square in a stack (using half of the longer white pieces); sew a 1½″ × 4¼″ piece to the right side of each orange square in the other stack (using the remainder of the longer white pieces). Press the seams open.

Sew half of longer white pieces to left sides of orange squares and half to right.

5. Sew a left-sided corner unit and a right-sided corner unit to opposite sides of every A unit, pinning carefully to align the seams. Press the seams open.

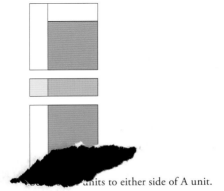

...nits to either side of A unit.

6. Sew a unit that you've just made to either side of every B unit. Press the seams open.

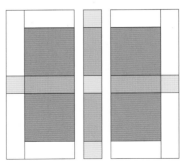

Assemble each block.

Assembly

1. Piece the blocks to the vertical divider strips and vertical edge pieces to form rows, referring to the quilt assembly diagram (page 49) as needed. Press the seams open.

2. Sew a horizontal divider strip to the bottom of each row *except* the bottom-most row. Press the seams open.

3. Align the rows precisely, using chalk to mark guidelines from the vertical divider seams down across the horizontal divider strips. Pin the next row at the chalk lines; then piece the rows together. Press the seams open.

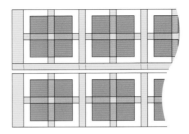

Mark chalk guidelines for alignment.

4. Attach the top and bottom panels. Press the seams open.

Finishing

For information on quilting, batting, and binding, see Quilting and Batting Options (page 102) and Binding (page 104).

1. Layer the top, batting, and backing; then quilt.

2. Trim the outer yellow border to 1¾″ wide (see Tip, page 47).

3. Bind.

SIZE VARIATIONS

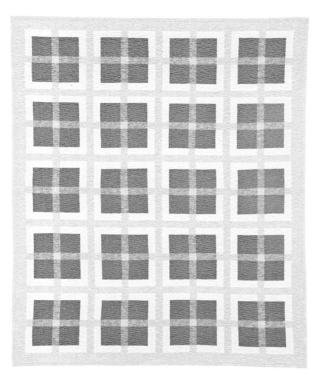

Wall/baby quilt, 40″ × 49″

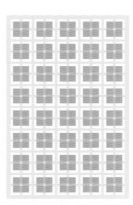

Napping quilt, 49″ × 78″

Full/queen quilt, 87″ × 106″

DESIGN

Fabric Selection

Just four fabrics are needed to make *Hello Sunshine*. From the start, we knew we wanted to create a sunny palette. Using crisp white for the field allowed sufficient contrast with the saturated yellow. The two oranges completed the palette.

White fabric

Yellow fabric

Light orange fabric

Medium orange fabric

Quilting

The complexity of the piecing and the delicacy of this transparency called for an allover quilting pattern. We chose white thread and a scalloped flower pattern to keep the quilting highly textured but not distracting.

Scalloped flower quilting pattern

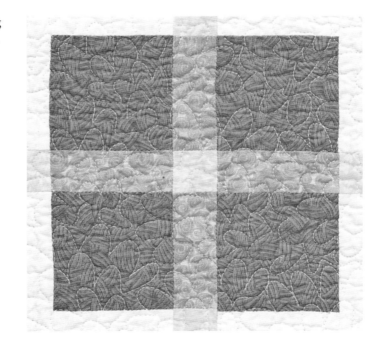

COLOR VARIATIONS

These variations show how a pattern that began as a baby quilt can be transformed into a throw for a tween girl, a masculine quilt for a man, or a breezy green quilt that would be at home in a seaside cottage.

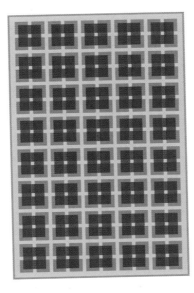
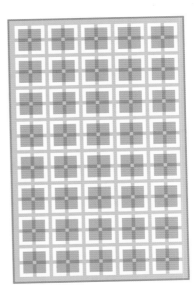

MADRAS

We've long admired the beauty of the colorful woven plaids of Madras, India. Our *Madras* quilt allows you to create your own festive, multicolored plaids. The construction mixes traditional cutting and assembly methods with strip sets to ease the handling of the narrow vertical bands.

Skill/Time ADVENTUROUS BEGINNER

The complex appearance of this quilt disguises its simple construction. The cutting and piecing are straightforward; you'll just need to take time to pin carefully.

Materials

All fabric calculations assume a width of 42".

	WALL/BABY	NAPPING	FULL/QUEEN
FINISHED SIZE	32" × 49"	50" × 80"	95" × 112"
MATERIALS NEEDED			
Green Fabric C for intersections	¼ yard	¾ yard	1¾ yards
Medium pink Fabric D for intersections	⅛ yard	¼ yard	½ yard
Light pink Fabric E for vertical stripes	¼ yard	½ yard	¾ yard
Yellow Fabric F for vertical stripes	½ yard	1½ yards	3 yards
Medium blue Fabric A for horizontal stripes	½ yard	1 yard	2¼ yards
Light blue Fabric B for field	¾ yard	1¾ yards	4 yards
Binding	½ yard	¾ yard	1 yard
Backing	1½ yards	5 yards	8½ yards*
Batting	38" × 55"	56" × 86"	101" × 118"

* Pieced crosswise

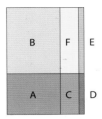

Fabric key

Tip We encourage you to experiment with fabric choices in this colorful quilt. If you are auditioning fabrics in a store, group the lighter fabrics together and the medium fabrics together. Hold the bolts upright and gently tap the bolt ends on a table. The rolled fabric will slide down, flush with the bolt end. You can now set the groups of bolts end to end, with their fabrics touching, to get a sense of how the plaid might appear.

Cutting

CUT	WALL/BABY	NAPPING	FULL/QUEEN
FROM GREEN FABRIC C			
	6 strips 2¼″ × 20″	10 strips 2¼″ × 35″	26 strips 2¼″ × 40″
FROM MEDIUM PINK FABRIC D			
	3 strips 1″ × 20″	5 strips 1″ × 35″	13 strips 1″ × 40″
FROM LIGHT PINK FABRIC E			
	3 strips 1″ × 36″	10 strips 1″ × 32″	22 strips 1″ × 40″
FROM YELLOW FABRIC F			
	6 strips 2¼″ × 36″	20 strips 2¼″ × 32″	44 strips 2¼″ × 40″
FROM MEDIUM BLUE FABRIC A			
5½″ × 4½″ pieces	16	42	110
FROM LIGHT BLUE FABRIC B			
5½″ × 7″ pieces	20	48	121

MAKING THE QUILT

Piecing the Strip Sets

	WALL/BABY	NAPPING	FULL/QUEEN
Green strip sets	3	5	13
Yellow strip sets	3	10	22

1. Using a ¼″ seam allowance, sew a green C strip to either side of each medium pink D strip. Don't worry if the ends don't align precisely; the strip sets have extra length built in for trimming later. Press the seams open.

Green strip set

2. Sew a yellow F strip to either side of each light pink E strip. Press the seams open.

Yellow strip set

Cutting the Strip Sets

CUT	WALL/ BABY	NAPPING	FULL/ QUEEN
FROM GREEN STRIP SETS			
4½″ × 4½″ blocks	12	35	100
FROM YELLOW STRIP SETS			
4½″ × 7″ blocks	15	40	110

1. Cut the green strip sets in 4½″ lengths to make the specified number of 4½″ × 4½″ blocks.

2. Cut the yellow strip sets in 7″ lengths to make the specified number of 4½″ × 7″ blocks.

Cut strip sets into blocks.

Assembly

1. Sew the blocks together in rows, alternating plain blocks and pieced blocks and following the quilt assembly diagram (to the right). Press the seams open.

2. Piece the rows together, pinning carefully through the seams first to ensure precise alignment. Press the seams open.

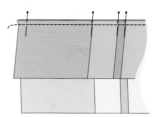

Pin to align seams.

Finishing

For information on quilting, batting, and binding, see Quilting and Batting Options (page 102) and Binding (page 104).

1. Layer the top, batting, and backing; then quilt.

2. Bind.

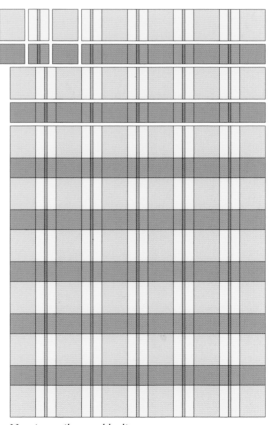

Napping quilt assembly diagram

SIZE VARIATIONS

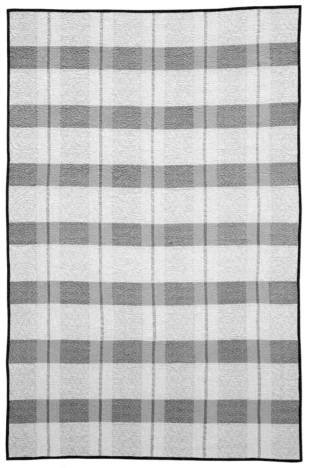

Napping quilt, 50″ × 80″

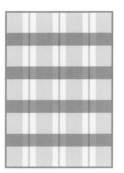

Wall/baby quilt, 32″ × 49″

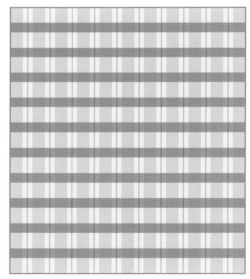

Full/queen quilt, 95″ × 112″

DESIGN

Fabric Selection

Madras relies on a somewhat literal color interpretation of transparency. The blue horizontal bands cross the yellow verticals to form green intersections. The pink accent strips become darker at the intersections.

Creating your own color palette is straightforward. Start by selecting three colors: the vertical band color, the horizontal band color, and the intersection color. Now find a lighter value of the horizontal band color to use as the field. Next, choose an accent color for the narrow vertical strip. Finally, find a slightly darker and desaturated (duller) variation of the accent color for the intersections.

These are the six fabrics we used:

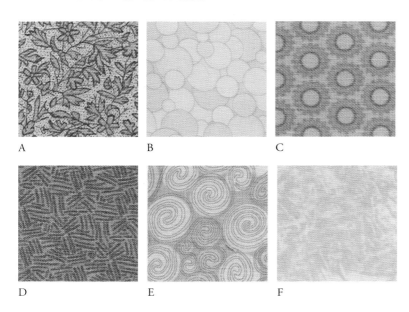

A

B

C

D

E

F

Quilting

The small freehand spiral quilting of *Madras* ties together the weave of the plaid. We chose a pale gray thread that blended well with the yellow, blues, green, and pinks.

Spiral quilting

COLOR VARIATIONS

Study these three colorful variations. You'll see that each was developed according to the steps described in Fabric Selection (page 59).

BUNGALOW

The simplicity of *Bungalow*'s repeating motif was inspired by geometric patterns of the 50s and 60s. This is an example of those "blue plus yellow doesn't have to make green" approaches to transparency. Instead of being literal by shifting in hue, the yellow bar simply shifts in value as it crosses through the blue.

Skill/Time ADVENTUROUS BEGINNER

Strip piecing makes *Bungalow* simple and speedy to put together, especially the full/queen version. The pattern does not require literal transparency, so the fabric selection is very open ended and forgiving.

Materials

All fabric calculations assume a width of 42″.

	WALL/BABY	NAPPING	FULL/QUEEN
FINISHED SIZE	40″ × 47″	51″ × 82″	92″ × 109″
MATERIALS NEEDED			
Green field fabric	1½ yards	4 yards	7 yards
Blue-gray fabric	½ yard	1 yard	2 yards
Light yellow fabric	¼ yard	½ yard	¾ yard
Orange fabric	¼ yard	½ yard	1¼ yards
Binding	½ yard	¾ yard	1 yard
Backing	1½ yards	5 yards	8½ yards*
Batting	46″ × 53″	57″ × 88″	98″ × 115″

* Pieced crosswise

Tip To align the rows, mark the center of the edge of each block. Our trick to speed this up was to cut a piece of cardstock the width of the block. We cut a small notch at the center of the edge. By laying this jig over each finished block, we could quickly chalk at the notch, leaving a perfect center mark. We made a smaller jig the width of the filler pieces between the blocks to mark their centers.

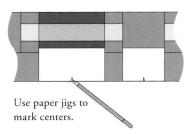

Use paper jigs to mark centers.

Cutting

CUT	WALL/BABY	NAPPING	FULL/QUEEN
FROM GREEN FIELD FABRIC			
Row end pieces, 6½″ × 4″	6	12	18
Between-block pieces, 4″ × 4″	11	33	93
Horizontal divider strips	6 strips 3″ × 33″	12 strips 3″ × 45″ *	16 strips 3″ × 81″ *
Top and bottom panels	2 pieces 4″ × 40″	2 pieces 3¾″ × 51½″ *	2 pieces 5¼″ × 92″ *
2 side panels	2 pieces 4″ × 40″	2 pieces 3¾″ × 76″ *	2 pieces 6″ × 100″ *
Strips for strip sets, 1½″ × 40″	4	10	22
FROM BLUE-GRAY FABRIC			
Strips for strip sets, 1½″ × 40″	6	16	38
FROM LIGHT YELLOW FABRIC			
Strips for strip sets, 2″ × 40″	2	5	11
FROM ORANGE FABRIC			
Strips for strip sets, 2″ × 40″	3	8	19

* Cut pieces marked with an asterisk from the lengthwise grain.

MAKING THE QUILT

Making the Strip Sets

	WALL/BABY	NAPPING	FULL/QUEEN
Blue-orange-blue strip sets	3	8	19
Green-yellow-green strip sets	2	5	11

1. Using a ¼″ seam allowance, sew a blue strip to either side of an orange strip to make a blue-orange-blue strip set. Press the seams open.

Make blue-orange-blue strip sets.

2. Repeat to make the required number of strip sets.

3. Sew a green strip to either side of a yellow strip to make a green-yellow-green strip set. Press the seams open.

Make green-yellow-green strip sets.

4. Repeat to make the required number of strip sets.

Making the Blocks

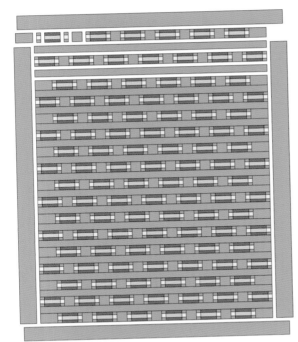

Full/queen quilt assembly diagram

	WALL/BABY	NAPPING	FULL/QUEEN
Blue-orange-blue center pieces, 6″ wide	18	46	110
Green-yellow-green end pieces, 2″ wide	36	92	220

1. Cut the blue-orange-blue strip sets into the required number of 6″ center pieces. Set these aside.

Cut center pieces.

2. Cut the green-yellow-green strip sets into the required number of 2″ end pieces. Set these aside.

Cut end pieces.

3. Sew an end piece to either side of each center piece. Press the seams open.

Finished block

Assembly

1. Sew together the end pieces, blocks, and between-block pieces to form rows, referring to the quilt assembly diagram (to the left) as needed. Press the seams open.

2. Sew a horizontal divider strip to the bottom of each row *except* the bottom-most row. Press the seams open.

3. Align the rows precisely; then piece them together. See Tip (page 63) on using a jig to mark the centers. Press the seams open.

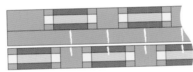

Chalk centers for alignment.

4. Attach the side panels. Press the seams open.

5. Attach the top and bottom panels. Press the seams open.

Finishing

For information on quilting, batting, and binding, see Quilting and Batting Options (page 102) and Binding (page 104).

1. Layer the top, batting, and backing; then quilt.

2. Bind.

SIZE VARIATIONS

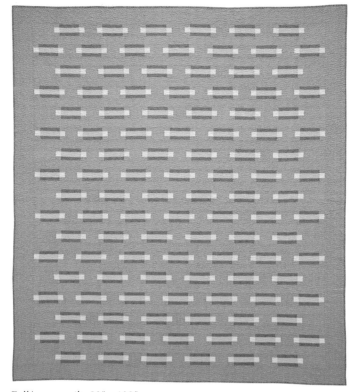

Full/queen quilt, 92″ × 109″

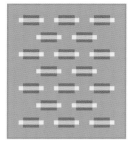

Wall/baby quilt, 40″ × 47″

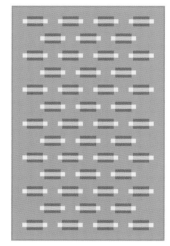

Napping quilt, 51″ × 82″

DESIGN

Fabric Selection

Prototyping the colors by cutting pieces roughly
to scale can save valuable time and fabric.

Field fabric

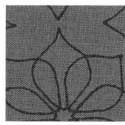

Blue fabric

Yellow fabric

Orange fabric

Quilting

We developed this freehand quilting pattern after studying the undulations of the grain in the old oak floorboards in our 1914 bungalow. Its horizontal flow works well with the proportions of this block.

Wood-grain quilting pattern

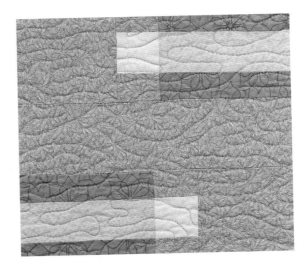

COLOR VARIATIONS

The first variation shows how swapping the green and orange fabrics transforms *Bungalow* from its original colorway. The middle variation shows an understated, monochromatic look. You can create an additional overlay of pattern by using multiple block colors, as in the last illustration.

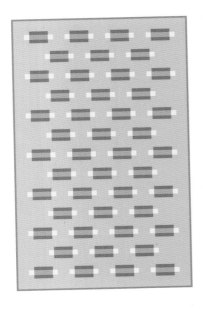
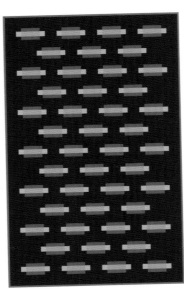

SMALL WORLD

The narrow horizontal bands in *Small World* create subtle transparency and unify the eclectic selection of fabrics. The stripes, wovens, paisleys, modern prints, and vintage reproductions create a scrappy yet contemporary look.

Skill/Time BEGINNER

Small World is simple to make. Just measure carefully and take your time cutting the 1″ bands to keep them even. Variety spices up this quilt, so have fun collecting fabrics.

Materials

All fabric calculations assume a width of 42″.

	WALL/BABY	NAPPING	FULL/QUEEN
FINISHED SIZE	44″ × 43″	52″ × 79″	88″ × 105″
MATERIALS NEEDED			
Dark blue band fabric	1½ yards* (¼ yard)	1¾ yards* (½ yard)	2¾ yards* (1 yard)
Medium blue band fabric	⅛ yard	¼ yard	1¾ yards* (½ yard)
Assorted multicolored fabrics	¾ yard total	2 yards total	3¾ yards total
Assorted oatmeal-colored fabrics	1¼ yards total	1¾ yards total	4 yards total
Binding	½ yard	¾ yard	1 yard
Backing	2¾ yards**	3¼ yards**	8¼ yards**
Batting	50″ × 49″	58″ × 85″	94″ × 111″

* Pieced crosswise

** The first quantity is for cutting the bands (see the cutting chart, page 70) from continuous yardage with the lengthwise grain. The second quantity (in parentheses) uses less fabric but requires piecing smaller segments to make the longer bands. We prefer cutting continuous bands even though it means buying more fabric. Seaming the bands creates a subtle visual distraction, which is especially evident if the bands are left unquilted. Still, if you find cutting continuous narrow bands for the full/queen size too challenging, feel free to piece shorter bands together.

Tip Take your time and maintain consistent seam allowances when you sew the narrow blue strips to the rows of squares. If your seam allowances vary by as little as ⅛″ the inconsistencies may be noticeable. Such variations may not show on a larger piece, but this finished strip is only ½″ wide, so uneven seam allowances may look sloppy.

Cutting

CUT	WALL/BABY	NAPPING	FULL/QUEEN
FROM DARK BLUE BAND FABRIC			
Full-width bands	3 strips 1″ × 44½″ *	7 strips 1″ × 52½″ *	9 strips 1″ × 88½″ *
Edge bands	4 strips 1″ × 8½″	12 strips 1″ × 8½″	16 strips 1″ × 16½″
FROM MEDIUM BLUE BAND FABRIC			
Center bands	2 strips 1″ × 28½″	6 strips 1″ × 36½″	8 strips 1″ × 56½″ *
FROM MULTICOLORED FABRICS			
4½″ × 4½″ squares	42	126	252
FROM OATMEAL-COLORED FABRICS			
4½″ × 4½″ squares	68	108	276

* Cut pieces marked with an asterisk from the lengthwise grain or piece them from shorter segments.

MAKING THE QUILT

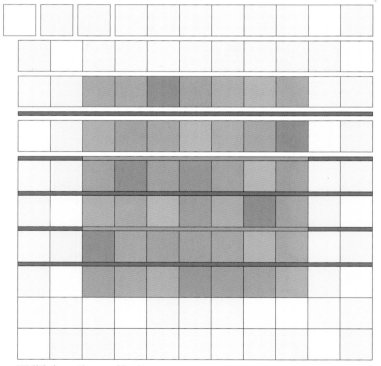

Wall/baby quilt assembly diagram

Assembly

1. Using a ¼″ seam allowance, sew a dark blue edge band to either side of each medium blue center band. Press the seams open.

2. Arrange the medium blue and oatmeal-colored squares, referring to the quilt assembly diagram (page 70). Step back at least 10 feet and rearrange squares as needed to achieve a pleasing composition.

3. Sew the squares into rows. Press the seams open.

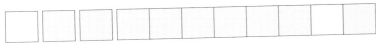

Sew rows.

4. Sew the pieced blue bands and dark blue bands between the rows of squares. Press the seams open.

Sew blue bands to rows.

5. Join the rows. You can align the rows visually without chalking because the blue bands are so narrow. Pin together the rows and then sew them. Press the seams open.

Finishing

For information on quilting, batting, and binding, see Quilting and Batting Options (page 102) and Binding (page 104).

1. Layer the top, batting, and backing; then quilt.

2. Bind.

SIZE VARIATIONS

Wall/baby quilt, 44″ × 43″

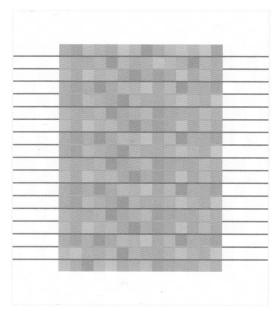

Full/queen quilt, 88″ × 105″

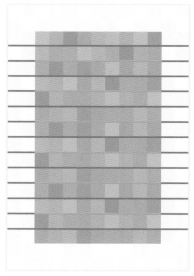

Napping quilt, 52″ × 79″

DESIGN

Fabric Selection

This is a great stash-buster quilt. We used each of the colored squares just once or twice. If you're making a larger size, consider asking your quilting friends if they could spare a few squares of fabric. Not only will this add to the scrappiness, but it will also add memories of your friends and their contributions to your quilting life. Because the oatmeal-colored squares draw less attention, we were able to have less variety, cutting multiple squares of each fabric.

This eclectic selection of fabrics includes stripes, wovens, paisleys, contemporary prints, and vintage reproductions.

What unifies them is that they are all desaturated—that is to say, none are bright—and that all have counterparts within the quilt. For instance, when we first added a striped fabric to the collection, it stood out. Once we added a second striped fabric, however, the first no longer drew attention to itself. We avoided fabrics containing pure white because they stood out among the softer palette of creams.

The most challenging fabric to pick was the binding. Oatmeal-colored fabrics blended with the field and didn't provide enough edge. We auditioned the light blue and dark blue fabrics used in the horizontal bands, but both were distracting and overwhelmed the subtle transparency. Finally we found a mustard-and-cream paisley that created a soft yet clear edge.

Multicolored fabrics

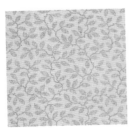

Oatmeal-colored fabrics

Dark blue band

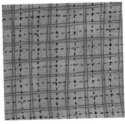

Medium blue band

Quilting

We left the narrow blue bands unquilted to accentuate their forms. We further differentiated the colored prints from the off-white field with different quilting. The field is densely quilted in an oval pebble pattern using off-white thread. The quilting in the prints corresponds to the parallel blue lines. It is a horizontal variation of a stipple done with neutral tan thread.

Horizontal stipple

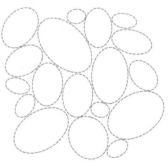

Oval pebbles

COLOR VARIATIONS

Consider how darker fabrics around the perimeter change the feel of the quilt by framing the center blocks. You may even want to explore color relationships without worrying about whether or not the lines create a sense of transparency.

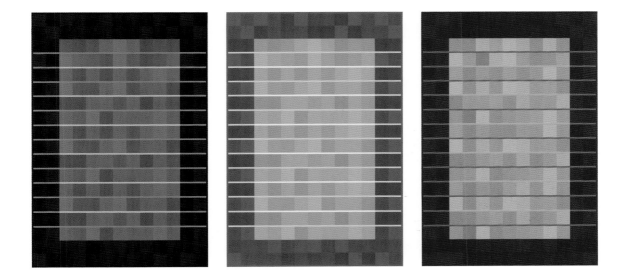

NEXT IN LINE

This handsome quilt defies the notion that all transparencies have to be light and airy. The link that joins the blocks unifies the varied gray fabrics. If you've collected a lot of a single hue over the years—blues or greens for instance—this is a great stash-buster quilt.

Skill/Time INTERMEDIATE

Next in Line has straightforward cutting and piecing, but you'll want to take your time choosing fabrics and matching points. Carefully matched points aid in the illusion that the blocks are linked together.

Materials

All fabric calculations assume a width of 42″.

	WALL/BABY	NAPPING	FULL/QUEEN
FINISHED SIZE	37″ × 46″	53″ × 81″	87″ × 104″
MATERIALS NEEDED			
Assorted gray block fabrics	¼ yard each of 6 fabrics	¼ yard each of 11 fabrics	½ yard each of 11 fabrics
Light connecting piece fabric	¼ yard	¾ yard	1¼ yards
Dark connecting piece fabric	⅛ yard	¼ yard	½ yard
Black field fabric	1¼ yards	3 yards*	5½ yards*
Binding	½ yard	¾ yard*	1 yard*
Backing	1½ yards	5 yards	8¼ yards**
Batting	43″ × 52″	59″ × 87″	93″ × 110″

* If you are binding a napping or full/queen quilt using the same fabric as the field fabric, you will have enough from the field fabric yardage and won't need to buy additional fabric for the binding.

** Pieced crosswise

Tip When selecting fabrics, note that the center rectangle fabric doesn't have to be exactly the color you'd get if you mixed the lighter and darker colors together. The overlapping rectangles provide the visual hint to expect the transparency, so concentrate on choosing the appropriate values to make the transparency convincing.

Cutting

CUT	WALL/BABY	NAPPING	FULL/QUEEN
FROM ASSORTED GRAY BLOCK FABRICS			
A pieces 2¼″ × 7¾″	48 pieces (8 each of 6 fabrics)	132 pieces (12 each of 11 fabrics)	286 pieces (26 each of all 11 fabrics)
B pieces 2¼″ × 3¼″	12 pieces (2 each of 6 fabrics)	44 pieces (4 each of 11 fabrics)	112 pieces (10 each of 9 fabrics, 11 each of 2 fabrics)
C pieces 2¼″ × 5½″	12 pieces (2 each of 6 fabrics)	22 pieces (2 each of 11 fabrics)	29 pieces (3 each of 9 fabrics, 1 each of 2 fabrics)
FROM LIGHTER CONNECTING PIECE FABRIC			
D pieces 2¼″ × 2¾″	36	110	253
FROM DARKER CONNECTING PIECE FABRIC			
E strips for strip sets	1 strip 2¼″ × 24″	2 strips 2¼″ × 40″	4 strips 2¼″ × 40″
FROM BLACK FIELD FABRIC			
F strips for strip sets	2 strips 2¼″ × 24″	4 strips 2¼″ × 40″	8 strips 2¼″ × 40″
Horizontal divider strips	5 strips 2¼″ × 31¾″	10 strips 2¼″ × 47¾″ *	13 strips 2¼″ × 79¾″ *
Top and bottom panels	3¼″ × 37¼″	3¼″ × 53¼″ *	4¼″ × 87¼″ *
2 side panels	3¼″ × 40¾″	3¼″ × 75¾″ *	4¼″ × 96¾″ *

* Cut pieces marked with an asterisk from the lengthwise grain.

MAKING THE QUILT

Making the Blocks

	WALL/BABY	NAPPING	FULL/QUEEN
End blocks	12	22	28
Center blocks	12	44	112

1. Using a ¼″ seam allowance, sew each gray C piece to a light D piece. Press the seams open.

Sew C to D.

2. Sew matching A pieces to the top and bottom of each C–D unit. Press the seams open. These will be the end blocks. If you are making the full/queen size, you will end up with 29 blocks, one more than you'll need. This will give you flexibility when laying out the quilt.

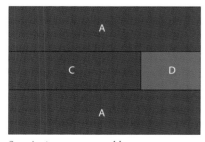

Sew A pieces to top and bottom.

3. Sew a light D piece to either side of each gray B piece. Press the seams open.

Sew D to B to D.

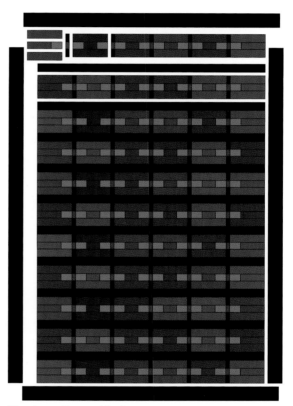

Napping quilt assembly diagram

4. Sew matching A pieces to the top and bottom of each D–B–D unit. Press the seams open. These will be the center blocks.

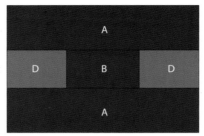

Sew A pieces to top and bottom.

Making Connecting Pieces

	WALL/BABY	NAPPING	FULL/QUEEN
Number of connecting pieces	18	55	126

1. Sew a black F strip to either side of each dark E strip. Press the seams open.

Make strip sets.

2. Cut the strip sets into the required number of 1¼"-wide connecting pieces.

Cut strip sets into pieces.

Assembly

1. Sew a connecting strip to one side of every center block, pinning carefully through the seams to ensure alignment. Press the seams open.

Sew connecting strips to center blocks.

2. Sew a connecting strip to one side of half of the end blocks, pinning carefully through the seams to ensure alignment. Press the seams open.

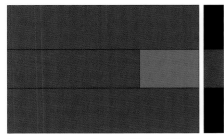

Sew connecting strips to half of end blocks.

3. Arrange the pieces, ensuring an even distribution of fabrics. Refer to the assembly diagram (page 79) as needed.

4. Sew the blocks into rows, pinning carefully through the seams to ensure alignment. Press the seams open.

5. Sew a horizontal divider strip to the bottom of each row *except* the bottom-most row. Press the seams open.

6. Align the rows, using chalk to mark guidelines from the vertical seams down across the horizontal divider strips. Pin the next row on the chalk lines; then piece the rows together. Press the seams open.

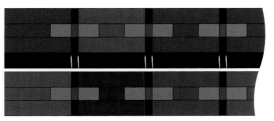

Mark chalk guidelines for alignment.

7. Sew on the side panels. Press the seams open.

8. Sew on the top and bottom panels. Press the seams open.

Finishing

For information on quilting, batting, and binding, see Quilting and Batting Options (page 102) and Binding (page 104).

1. Layer the top, batting, and backing; then quilt.

2. Bind.

SIZE VARIATIONS

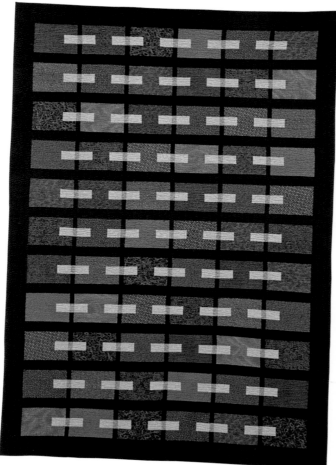

Napping quilt, 53″ × 81″

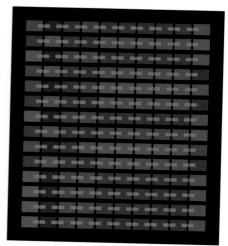

Full/queen quilt, 87″ × 104″

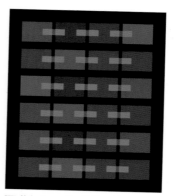

Wall/baby quilt, 37″ × 46″

DESIGN

Fabric Selection

The challenge in selecting these fabrics was achieving unity among the grays. We used predominantly cool grays with blue or green undertones. The light and dark connecting piece fabrics are cool as well. For these, we chose two fabrics of the same hue but of different values (a lighter fabric and a darker fabric). It was helpful to look at them against the field fabric to ensure that there would be enough contrast among the blocks and with the field fabric itself.

The fabrics for the gray blocks are all tone-on-tone prints that hide seams well, so each block reads as a single piece, not three strips sewn together.

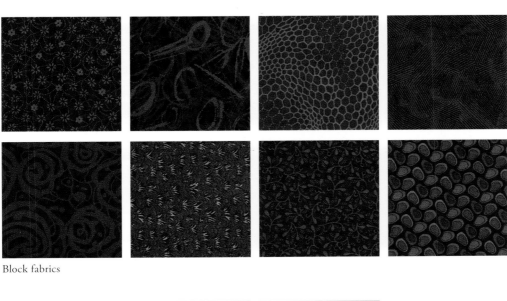

Block fabrics

Light connecting piece fabric

Dark connecting piece fabric

Black solid field

SWEET TALK

The informal approach to transparency in *Sweet Talk* allows the use of prints in many scales. By using dozens of different fabrics carefully grouped by hue and value, we achieved a scrappy, casual feel.

Skill/Time BEGINNER

Large pieces simplify the cutting and piecing, making this quilt fairly quick to piece.

Materials

All fabric calculations assume a width of 42".

	WALL/BABY	NAPPING	FULL/QUEEN
FINISHED SIZE	32" × 47"	55" × 86"	88" × 103"
MATERIALS NEEDED			
Assorted light prints	½ yard total	1 yard total	1¾ yards total
Assorted medium prints	¼ yard total	¾ yard total	1½ yards total
Assorted dark prints	¼ yard total	¾ yard total	1½ yards total
Solid white field fabric	1½ yards	3½ yards	5 yards
Binding	½ yard	¾ yard	1 yard
Backing	1½ yards	5¼ yards	8¼ yards*
Batting	38" × 53"	61" × 92"	94" × 109"

* Pieced crosswise

Tip   When you sew together the rows, maintain a consistent ¼" seam allowance so you don't accidentally truncate the tips of the on-point squares. Use pink thread to sew the blocks together, but when it comes time to sew the rows to each other, switch to white thread so the stitching and thread ends don't show through the white field fabric.

Cutting

Trace the A and B template patterns (page 109) onto template plastic. Cut them out and label them. Put a piece of double-faced tape or a loop of clear tape on the back of each to keep it in place as you cut.

CUT	WALL/BABY	NAPPING	FULL/QUEEN
FROM ASSORTED LIGHT PRINTS			
4½″ × 4½″ squares	18	60	112
FROM ASSORTED MEDIUM PRINTS			
4½″ × 4½″ squares	6	36	84
FROM ASSORTED DARK PRINTS			
4½″ × 4½″ squares	6	36	84
FROM WHITE FIELD FABRIC			
Small triangles, using Template A	12	72	168
Large triangles, using Template B	12	24	28
Divider strips	2 strips 2¼″ × 23¼″	5 strips 2¼″ × 45¾″ *	6 strips 2¼″ × 79¾″ *
2 side panels	5″ × 38″	5″ × 77¼″ *	5″ × 90¼″ *
Top and bottom panels	5″ × 32¼″	5″ × 54¾″ *	7″ × 88¾″ *

* Cut pieces marked with an asterisk from the lengthwise grain.

MAKING THE QUILT

Napping quilt assembly diagram

Assembly

1. Arrange the pieces, referring to the quilt assembly diagram (above) as needed. Rearrange pieces if you notice awkward adjacencies or if any transparencies are too subtle. Number the pieces with chalk to keep them in order when taking them from the layout area to the sewing machine.

2. Using a ¼″ seam allowance, sew the diagonal sub-units of each row as shown in the quilt assembly diagram. Press the seams open.

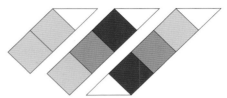

Diagonal sub-units

3. Referring to the quilt assembly diagram, sew the first and last 2 diagonal sub-units of each row together, and then sew these to a large triangle. Press the seams open.

4. Sew the remaining diagonal sub-units together and then attach the remaining large triangles at each end. Press the seams open.

5. Sew the rows and dividing strips together. Press the seams open.

6. Sew the side panels to the pieced center. Press the seams open.

7. Sew the top and bottom panels to the pieced center. Press the seams open.

Finishing

For information on quilting, batting, and binding, see Quilting and Batting Options (page 102) and Binding (page 104).

1. Layer the top, batting, and backing; then quilt.

2. Bind.

SIZE VARIATIONS

Napping quilt, 55″ × 86″

Wall/baby quilt, 32″ × 47″

Full/queen quilt, 88″ × 103″

DESIGN

Fabric Selection

At first glance this appears to be a pink-and-white quilt. Look closely, though, and you'll see reds, oranges, salmons, and even bits of green and purple, especially among the darker fabrics. We began by dividing our pink stash into three value piles: light, medium, and dark. We soon noticed that many of our darker fabrics were actually multicolored. While any single multicolored fabric might be distracting, when combined with other similarly patterned fabrics, the group works.

Light pinks

Medium pinks

Dark pinks

Quilting

Pieced in pinks and white, *Sweet Talk* is unmistakably a girly-girl quilt. The quilted daisy chain pattern builds on this appearance while creating visual interest in the expansive white field. If you choose to make this in a more masculine palette, a simple stipple would work well.

Daisy chain quilting

COLOR VARIATIONS

Sweet Talk is easily visualized in monochromatic variations such as the blue and white shown here. Now imagine it with additional hues, such as these desert blues, greens, and tans, or in the colorful prismatic variation.

TARTAN

Tartan transforms six shades of blue into a stunning plaid. We used a clever strip assembly method for the piecing. If you're used to traditional blocks, this will be a novel approach. Read through the entire pattern to visualize this innovative method that creates a bold, graphic plaid.

Skill/Time ADVANCED

This is a good project for an experienced quilter interested in learning new construction methods. Labeling and organization will help you keep the different blues sorted. Careful craftsmanship will contribute greatly to the illusion of a woven plaid. Take your time to ensure accurate cutting, pinning, and piecing, and your points will match well. If you are drawn to the plaid look but want to try an easier pattern first, consider starting with our *Madras* quilt (page 54).

Materials

All fabric calculations assume a width of 42".

	WALL/BABY	NAPPING	FULL/QUEEN
FINISHED SIZE	42" × 44"	54" × 87"	88" × 104"
MATERIALS NEEDED			
For lighter columns			
Blue field Fabric C	1½ yards	2½ yards	5¾ yards
Light blue Fabric A	½ yard	1¼ yards	1¼ yards
Dark blue fabric for narrow horizontal band D	⅛ yard	¼ yard	¼ yard
For darker columns			
Deep blue Fabric E	½ yard	1¾ yards	1¾ yards
Medium blue Fabric B	⅜ yard	1¼ yards	1¼ yards
Darkest blue fabric for narrow horizontal band F	⅛ yard	¼ yard	¼ yard
Binding	½ yard	¾ yard	1 yard
Backing	2¾ yards*	5¼ yards	8¼ yards*
Batting	48" × 50"	60" × 93"	94" × 110"

* Pieced crosswise

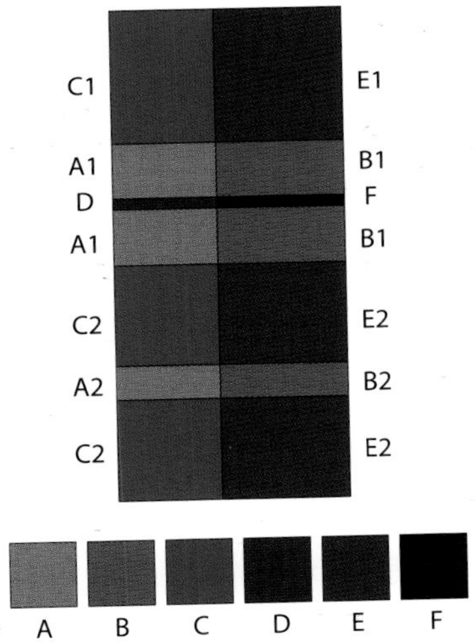

Top corner of plaid with fabrics labeled A–F

Tip *Tartan* is assembled in strips rather than in traditional blocks. We've broken up the assembly into upper and lower halves for the napping and full/queen sizes to avoid having you work with overly long strips that are prone to warping and stretching. We found it helpful to sew *Tartan* in longer sewing sessions to keep the order of the strips straight.

Cutting

CUT	WALL/BABY	NAPPING	FULL/QUEEN
FROM BLUE FIELD FABRIC C (CUT AND LABEL)			
Top and bottom panels	5½" × 42"	3" × 54" *	11½" × 88" *
2 side panels	5½" × 34"	3" × 41½" for upper side panels; 3" × 41" for lower side panels	11½" × 41½" for upper side panels; 11½" × 41" for lower side panels
C1 pieces	2 pieces 6½" × 21"	2 pieces 6½" × 31"	2 pieces 6½" × 41"
C2 pieces	2 pieces 5" × 21"	8 pieces 5" × 31"	8 pieces 5" × 41"
FROM LIGHT BLUE FABRIC A			
A1 pieces	4 pieces 3" × 21"	10 pieces 3" × 31"	10 pieces 3" × 41"
A2 pieces	1 piece 2" × 21"	4 pieces 2" × 31"	4 pieces 2" × 41"
FROM DARK BLUE FABRIC D			
D pieces	2 pieces 1" × 21"	5 pieces 1" × 31"	5 pieces 1" × 41"
FROM DEEP BLUE FABRIC E			
E1 pieces	2 pieces 6½" × 16"	2 pieces 6½" × 25"	2 pieces 6½" × 34"
E2 pieces	2 pieces 5" × 16"	8 pieces 5" × 25"	8 pieces 5" × 34"
FROM MEDIUM BLUE FABRIC B			
B1 pieces	4 pieces 3" × 16"	10 pieces 3" × 25"	10 pieces 3" × 34"
B2 pieces	1 piece 2" × 16"	4 pieces 2" × 25"	4 pieces 2" × 34"
FROM DARKEST BLUE FABRIC F			
F pieces	2 pieces 1" × 16"	5 pieces 1" × 25"	5 pieces 1" × 34"

* Cut pieces marked with an asterisk from the lengthwise grain.

MAKING THE QUILT

The full/queen and napping versions of this quilt are pieced in two halves to make the piecing and cutting more manageable. This method also minimizes bowing of the strip sets. All of these strip sets are 1″ wider than needed to allow for slightly ragged edges to be trimmed flush. The following illustrations show the assembly of a full/queen quilt. Use ¼″ seam allowances.

Piecing the Strip Sets

WALL/BABY	NAPPING	FULL/QUEEN
Light strip sets		
C1, A1, D, A1, C2, A2, C2, A1, D, A1, C1	*Upper set, from top down:* C1, A1, D, A1, C2, A2, C2, A1, D, A1, C2, A2, C2, A1, D	*Upper set, from top down:* C1, A1, D, A1, C2, A2, C2, A1, D, A1, C2, A2, C2, A1, D
	Lower set, from top down: A1, C2, A2, C2, A1, D, A1, C2, A2, C2, A1, D, A1, C1	*Lower set, from top down:* A1, C2, A2, C2, A1, D, A1, C2, A2, C2, A1, D, A1, C1
Dark strip sets		
E1, B1, F, B1, E2, B2, E2, B1, F, B1, E1	*Upper set, from top down:* E1, B1, F, B1, E2, B2, E2, B1, F, B1, E2, B2, E2, B1, F	*Upper set, from top down:* E1, B1, F, B1, E2, B2, E2, B1, F, B1, E2, B2, E2, B1, F
	Lower set, from top down: B1, E2, B2, E2, B1, F, B1, E2, B2, E2, B1, F, B1, E1	*Lower set, from top down:* B1, E2, B2, E2, B1, F, B1, E2, B2, E2, B1, F, B1, E1

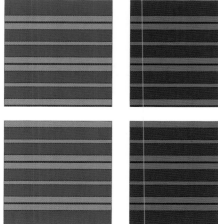

Strip sets for full/queen quilt

Cutting the Strip Sets

CUT	WALL/BABY	NAPPING	FULL/QUEEN
FROM LIGHT SETS			
	4 columns 5″ wide	6 columns 5″ wide from both upper and lower sets	8 columns 5″ wide from both upper and lower sets
FROM DARK SETS			
	2 columns 6″ wide and 1 column 3″ wide	3 columns 6″ wide and 2 columns 3″ wide from both upper and lower sets	4 columns 6″ wide and 3 columns 3″ wide from both upper and lower sets

Cut the upper and lower strip sets into columns.

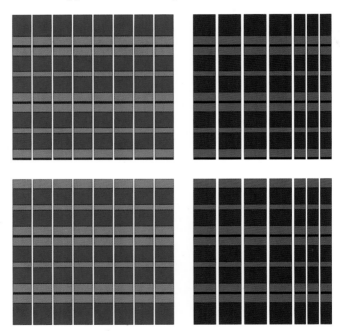

Cut strip sets into columns.

Assembly

1. Lay out the columns, alternating light, wide dark, light, narrow dark, as shown in the assembly diagram (below right). The full/queen and napping sizes will be laid out in upper and lower halves to make the assembly more manageable.

2. Piece together the columns, pinning carefully through the seams first to ensure precise alignment. Press the seams open.

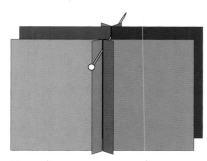

Pin to align seams.

3. Sew on the side panels. The full/queen and napping sizes will have side panels on the upper and lower halves. Press the seams open.

4. Sew on the top and bottom panels. Press the seams open.

5. If you are making the full/queen or napping sizes, sew the top section to the bottom section, pinning carefully to ensure precise alignment. Press the seam open.

Finishing

For information on quilting, batting, and binding, see Quilting and Batting Options (page 102) and Binding (page 104).

1. Layer the top, batting, and backing; then quilt.

2. Bind.

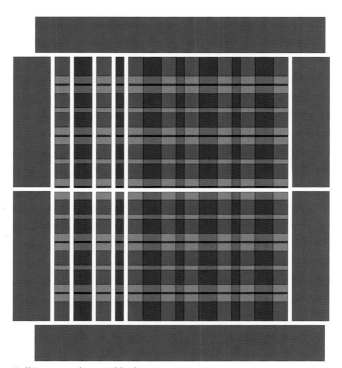

Full/queen quilt assembly diagram

SIZE VARIATIONS

Full/queen quilt, 88″ × 104″

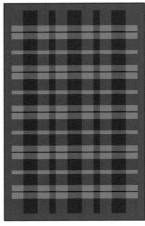

Wall/baby quilt, 42″ × 44″

Napping quilt, 54″ × 87″

DESIGN

Fabric Selection

You'll need different values of the same color for *Tartan.* We began by assembling more than the six we needed. We started with about a dozen or so and then removed fabrics that stood out either because they were slightly green or violet or perhaps because the patterns clashed with others. Here are the six fabrics we used:

A

B

C

D

E

F

You'll see that Fabrics B and C are similar in value, yet B appears brighter because it is more saturated (intense in color) than C. This subtle increase in saturation adds depth to the plaid and draws attention to the overlap of the horizontal and vertical bands.

Once you've selected fabrics, tape a small swatch of each to a sheet of paper and label them A–F. This will help you keep the fabrics straight as you follow the cutting and piecing instructions.

Quilting

We did not want the quilting to compete with the beauty of the colorwork, so we chose a blue-gray thread. The simple stipple flattens the quilt, bringing out the effect of overlapping horizontal and vertical bands.

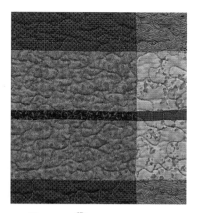

Stipple quilting

COLOR VARIATIONS

These monochromatic variations show how *Tartan* can be easily adapted to any hue. The advice in Fabric Selection (starting on previous page) will guide you through the process of picking a hue and determining which values are needed to make the transparency convincing.

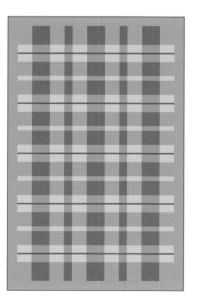
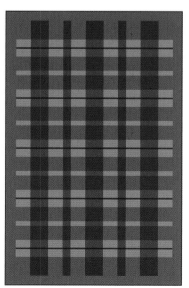

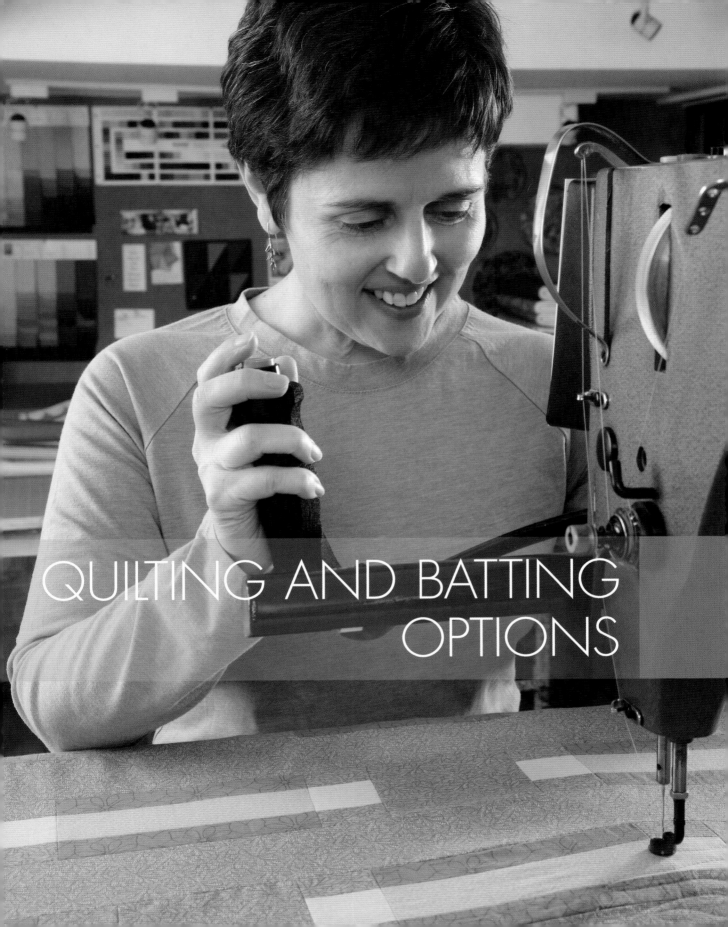

QUILTING AND BATTING
OPTIONS

QUILTING

By now you've carefully chosen the right fabrics and assembled your transparency, so you'll want to make sure that you quilt it in a manner that enhances your colorwork rather than detracting from it. In general, the simpler the quilting, the better. The transparencies are the stars of these quilts, so the quilting should be subservient to them. In bolder quilts, a lot of fancy threads and quilting patterns can add cheer, but in these quilts they would visually compete with the colorwork.

As for the color of thread to use in the quilting, look for desaturated thread colors. Then look at the lightest and darkest fabrics in the quilt. Choose a desaturated color that is halfway in value between the lightest and darkest color. Switching threads is fine, but be sure that any quilting enhances the colorwork instead of competing with it. This is a case of "less is more."

BATTING

All the quilts in this book were made with Quilters Dream 100% cotton batting in the Request loft (by Quilters Dream Batting), which is Quilters Dream's lightest-weight batting. We tell you this because when we lecture at quilt guilds, it is invariably the first question we are asked. We have no relationship with Quilters Dream; we just love the company's batting. The crinkly texture you see in our quilts is from the combination of this batting, dense quilting, and machine washing and drying our quilts. Although we prewash all our fabric prior to starting any project, we do wash the piece again after completion. The batting shrinks when dried on low heat, producing the pleasing crinkle.

Some of our clients prefer heavier lofts of batting, so we have used all the Quilters Dream 100% cotton lofts and recommend them all. We often use the densest loft, Supreme, for projects in public buildings or in homes where there are acoustic issues. In large rooms where there are a lot of hard surfaces, a wall quilt with the Supreme batting decreases echoes.

We often use Quilters Dream Wool and Quilters Dream Puff as well for projects in our own home. Dream Wool can be dried in the dryer on low and shrinks a bit as well. It is warmer than cotton but not as warm as Dream Puff. Dream Puff is synthetic, so it does not shrink at all but is extremely warm. You will not get the crinkly look with this or any other polyester or polyester blend, but with Dream Puff your toes will be toasty.

BINDING

We used the following single-step machine-binding technique to finish all the quilts in this book. All the bindings were made from strips cut with the crosswise grain (straight across from selvage to selvage), not on the bias (diagonal to the grain). We do not feel that it is necessary to cut on the bias if the quilt edge is straight. Cutting from selvage to selvage saves both time and money. This binding method requires just one tool: a bias tape maker. Our favorite is the Clover brand 1″ (25mm) bias tape maker. It transforms 2″ strips into ½″ finished binding.

If you are interested in learning about pillowcase binding or the more traditional hand-and-machine method, you will find complete instructions in our book *Quilts Made Modern*.

CUTTING THE BINDING STRIPS

1. Calculate the perimeter of the quilt and add 12″. For a 55″ × 75″ quilt, for example, this would be 55″ + 75″ + 55″ + 75″ + 12″ = 272″. This is the total length of binding needed.

2. Divide this by 40″ (the length of strips cut from selvage to selvage). Round up the result to determine the number of strips you need to cut. In this case, 272″ ÷ 40″ = 6.8, which you round up to 7 strips.

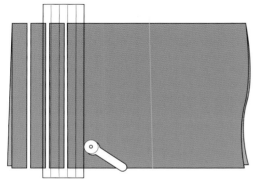

Fold fabric in half with selvages together and cut strips with crosswise grain.

ASSEMBLING THE BINDING STRIPS

1. Pin the right sides of 2 binding strips together at right angles and sew across diagonally.

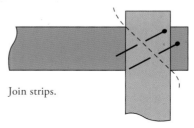

Join strips.

2. Sew the remaining strips together to form a continuous strip.

3. Trim the seam allowances to ¼″.

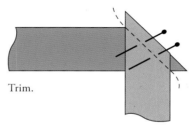

Trim.

4. Press open the seams to avoid bulges in the binding.

PREPARING THE BINDING

1. Cut an end of the continuous binding strip to a taper and insert it into the bias tape maker. Working on an ironing board, pull the strip through the tool, pressing the finished strip edges together in the center with light steam. As you encounter seams in the binding strip, make sure they are open and ease them through the tool.

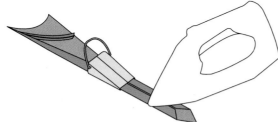

Press as you pull strip through tool.

2. Press the binding in half lengthwise to make a ½″ binding, setting with light steam.

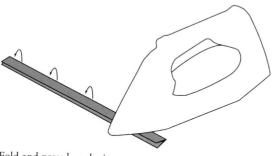

Fold and press lengthwise.

3. Square off the tapered end.

ATTACHING THE BINDING

1. With the front of the quilt facing up, start 6″ beyond a corner and wrap the folded binding around the raw edge of the quilt so it is snug. Pin the binding in place up to the next corner.

2. Leaving the first few inches of binding unsewn, stitch ⅛″ from the inner edge of the binding. Use your left hand to guide the quilt under the presser foot and your right hand to keep the binding snug against the quilt, sewing all the way to the corner. Lift the presser foot and cut the thread.

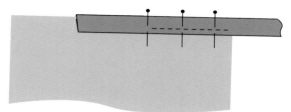

Fit binding on quilt and sew.

3. To miter the binding at the corner, hold the quilt in your left hand. Place your right thumb inside the binding strip and fold it open, creasing it at a 45° angle on the front and back.

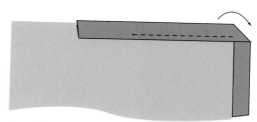

Open binding.

4. Fold the binding back toward the quilt, making crisp, finger-pressed miters on the front and back. Fit the raw edge of the quilt fully into the folded binding and pin in place to the next corner. You may find that with practice you can keep the binding snug enough without pinning. Backtack the mitered corner and then sew the binding 1/8" from the inner edge to the next corner.

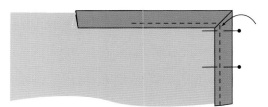

Fold and sew.

5. Repeat until you come to the last corner. Lift the presser foot and cut the thread.

6. Trim the free end of the binding so that it overlaps 1/2" with the beginning.

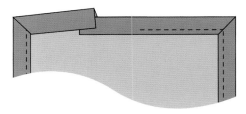

Trim, leaving 1/2" overlap.

7. Sew the ends together using a 1/4" seam allowance. Refold the binding in place, finger-pressing to crease.

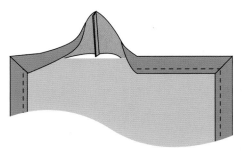

Sew ends.

8. Miter the last corner and continue sewing the binding until you overlap the first stitching. Backtack to reinforce.

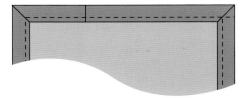

Finish sewing.

If you find that your stitching missed the binding on the back or if your binding separates from the quilt, it means you didn't keep it snugly and evenly wrapped around the quilt edge as you sewed. You might find it helpful to pin the binding in place until you get the hang of it. You'll be able to overcome these problems with a bit of practice.

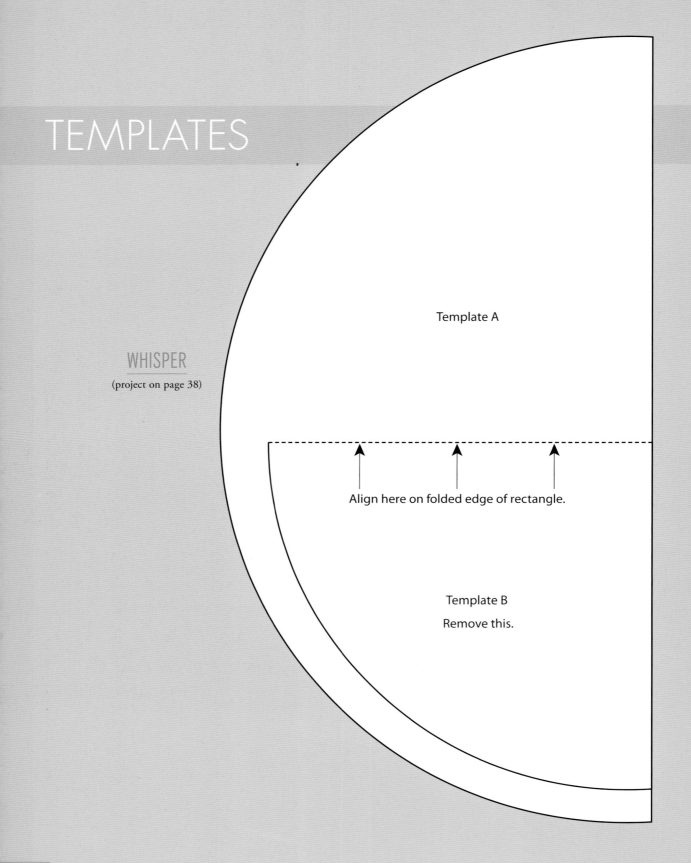

TEMPLATES

Template A

WHISPER

(project on page 38)

Align here on folded edge of rectangle.

Template B

Remove this.

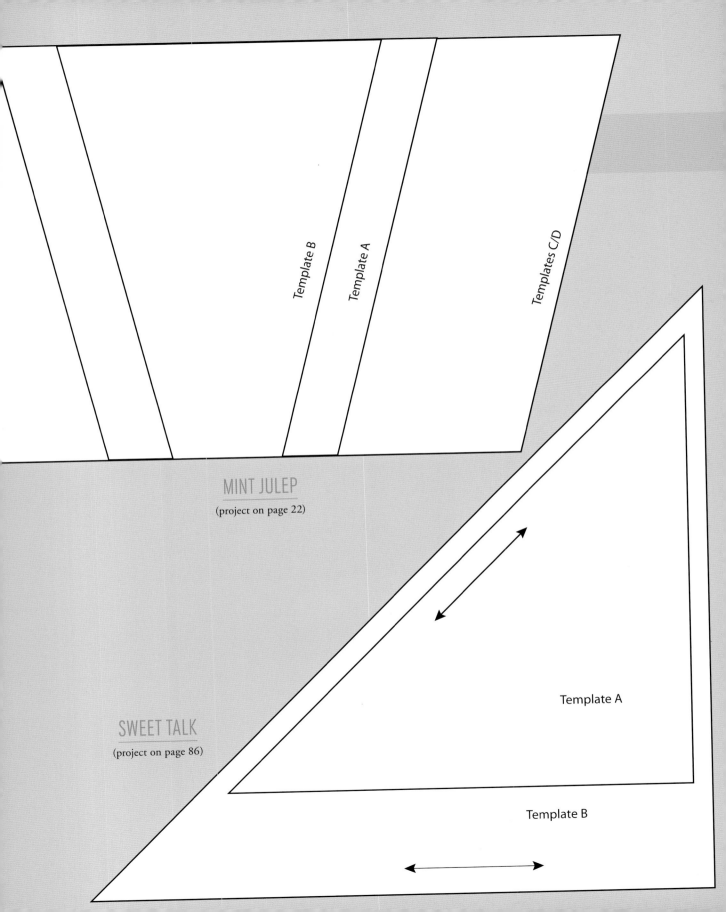

Template B

Template A

Templates C/D

MINT JULEP

(project on page 22)

SWEET TALK

(project on page 86)

Template A

Template B

RESOURCES

By the authors:

Modern Quilt Studio

www.modernquiltstudio.com

Our website offers more patterns, fabric, and the supplies mentioned in this book.

Craft Nectar   www.craftnectar.com

Weeks writes about design, inspiration, and quilts. Modern Quilt Studio also posts free patterns on Craft Nectar.

Modern Quilt Studio Fan Page on Facebook

www.facebook.com/pages/Modern-Quilt-Studio/206021399463625

Here you'll find frequent posts about new patterns and where we'll be teaching, as well as sneak peeks at what we're working on.

Other favorite resources:

American Patchwork & Quilting magazine

www.allpeoplequilt.com

This magazine has a wealth of tips and often features our latest patterns.

From Fiber to Fabric

www.ctpub.com

This is the seminal book for quilters by Harriet Hargrave on understanding the manufacturing and care of quilting fabrics. It is available from C&T Publishing as a downloadable eBook or a Print-on-Demand (POD) edition.

International Quilt Study Center & Museum

www.quiltstudy.org

This website has a wealth of information about traditional and antique quilts.

Jim White Photography

www.jimwhitephoto.com

All the styled shots in this book were taken by Jim.

The Modern Quilt Guild

www.themodernquiltguild.com

This blog provides information and inspiration for modern quilt guilds around the United States and guidance on how to start one in your area.

Quilts and More magazine

www.allpeoplequilt.com

Several of our beginner quilts and other sewing projects have appeared in *Quilts and More.*

The Textile Museum

www.textilemuseum.org

This museum offers guidelines for caring for antique and fragile textiles (see www.textilemuseum.org/care/brochures/guidelines.htm).

True Up   www.trueup.net

This is an informative blog about fabric.

Whip Up   www.whipup.net

This blog boasts links to vast numbers of free patterns and tutorials for quilts as well as other crafts.

ABOUT THE AUTHORS

Weeks Ringle and Bill Kerr are full-time professional quilt-makers and co-founders of Modern Quilt Studio, previously known as FunQuilts, a contemporary quilt design studio. Weeks and Bill bring a modern twist to the great American quilting tradition with decades of quiltmaking experience and graduate design degrees. They create innovative, museum-quality quilts that bring a warm touch to homes, offices, public spaces, and commercial settings.

Their work has been featured widely in the national press, including *O, The Oprah Magazine*; *Metropolitan Home*; *Time*; *The New York Times*; *Interior Design*; *Dwell*; and *Country Living*. They are the authors of numerous books on contemporary quilting, including *Quilts Made Modern, Quiltmaker's Color Workshop,* and *The Modern Quilt Workshop*. Their innovative patterns are often featured in *American Patchwork & Quilting*.

Also by Weeks Ringle and Bill Kerr:

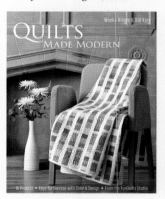

Available as an eBook

In addition to creating one-of-a-kind quilts, they have developed bedding and textiles for Crate and Barrel and have designed more than 100 original fabrics that have been sold in more than 15 countries. Their Many Hands Blankies project employs developmentally disabled adults in Chicago. For every 10 quilts they sell, they donate a quilt to charity. Recent donations have gone to the Respiratory Health Association of Metropolitan Chicago, West Suburban PADS (an organization that aims to provide shelter for the homeless), and Old Town School of Folk Music.

Bill also teaches design at Dominican University, and Weeks writes about craft and creativity on her blog, Craft Nectar (www.craftnectar.com). They live with their daughter in Oak Park, Illinois.

Great Titles and Products

from C&T PUBLISHING *and* stashBOOKS.

STUDIO COLOR WHEEL
28" × 28" Double-Sided Poster
JOEN WOLFROM

Ultimate 3-in-1 **COLOR TOOL**

Quilt Label Collective
Over 150 Designs to Customize, Print & Embellish

Bags the Modern Classics
Sue Kim
Totes, Hobos, Satchels & More
19 Projects • 75+ Bags

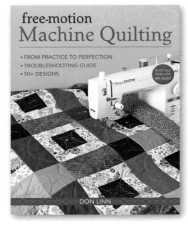

free-motion **Machine Quilting**
• FROM PRACTICE TO PERFECTION
• TROUBLESHOOTING GUIDE
• 50+ DESIGNS
DON LINN

ORGANIZING SOLUTIONS for Every Quilter
An Illustrated Guide to the Space of Your Dreams
Carolyn Woods

Available at your local retailer or **www.ctpub.com** *or* **800-284-1114**

For a list of other fine books from C&T Publishing, visit our website to view our catalog online.

C&T PUBLISHING, INC.

P.O. Box 1456
Lafayette, CA 94549
800-284-1114

Email: ctinfo@ctpub.com
Website: www.ctpub.com

C&T Publishing's professional photography services are now available to the public. Visit us at www.ctmediaservices.com.

Tips and Techniques can be found at www.ctpub.com > Consumer Resources > Quiltmaking Basics: Tips & Techniques for Quiltmaking & More

For quilting supplies:

COTTON PATCH

1025 Brown Ave.
Lafayette, CA 94549
Store: 925-284-1177
Mail order: 925-283-7883

Email: CottonPa@aol.com
Website: www.quiltusa.com

Note: Fabrics used in the quilts shown may not be currently available, as fabric manufacturers keep most fabrics in print for only a short time.